What's Your
Angel's Name

and what does it look like?

Kent Simpson, *Prophetic Pastor*

Foreword

Kent Simpson started talking about angels when angels weren't popular. For some of us, it's hard to imagine a time when supernatural things were too "out there" to preach on. The last twenty years have seen an explosion of super hero movies, vampire romances, and sorcery schools, all while having a mindset that this is acceptable to push toward our children.

God knew this season was coming, which is why many years ago He started introducing the subject of angels to the church. We need the experiences Kent shares in this book to equip us for the angelic and demonic encounters we should expect in the next era. I know that for me, the encounters I've had during my lifetime have sometimes confused me. What did I see, exactly? What did it mean? When I hear stories from the "Professionals of the Faith" that have been around longer than I have, it helps me understand my Father even more, especially when the experiences are told in story form, as Kent loves to do. When he shares them, the movie of his life plays in my head and it becomes an example I can follow.

Kent has been a pioneer in the prophetic movement of the last several decades. I believe God has used him to ruffle a few feathers and to tip people out of the prophetic boxes they've put themselves into. Part of a prophet's job description is to broach subjects that stretch the Body of Christ for the purpose of advancing God's Kingdom. After all, if we call ourselves sons of God, being corrected and disciplined by Him (a lot of times through His vessels) is part of the package.

"We have had human fathers who corrected us, and we paid them respect. Shall we not much more readily be in subjection to the Father of spirits and live?" (Heb. 12:9).

God is our God. He is also the God of the spirits. In His eyes, there is no segregation; we are all one big team, even when we don't see it, and even if we refuse to believe it's true. For the supernatural showdown that's coming, it would be extremely beneficial to us to learn what God is trying to teach us in this season regarding angels.

Foreword by Jennifer Ryan, an inspired writer and revelator who works in association with Kent Simpson and Prophetic Ministries Today.

Contents

———— ✳ ————

Chapter 1

Jesus and Angels

Angels, His Ministering Spirits

M inistering spirits are angels sent to minister *for* us, not just *to* us. When you gave your life to Jesus Christ, an angel was appointed unto you. That angel went before the face of God and reported your name to Him. These ministering spirits are waiting for you to yield unto the will of Jesus Christ so that He may dispatch them on your behalf to minister for you.

To each and every one of us there is at least one angel appointed as a guardian to watch over us, but there are more angels that are to be dispatched by the word of God. Jesus had thousands of angels at His disposal, and they ministered for Him, but then Jesus says in John 14:12 that "Greater works you will do!"

If you have more than one angel, you may find that something is working in your life that you truly could not have done on your own. You do not have the intellect to comprehend what God will do through you as He appoints an angel to minister for you. There are testimonials of people who knew they were supposed to die years ago. Their lives were spared for a purpose by angels who were watching over them until it was their appointed time to be with the Lord.

How do we obtain these angels? How do we receive the appointment of these angels? If we do not pray to them or worship them, how do we get their assistance as promised to us in Hebrews 1:14: "Are they not all ministering spirits sent forth to minister for those who will inherit salvation?"

It all begins with the impartation of a spiritual gift from the Holy Spirit. When you received the baptism of the Holy Spirit, there was a gift appointed unto you. That gift is still there with you. If you look back and recall when you received the baptism of Jesus, not only of water, but of the Spirit (according to Acts 1:5), then you will see that there was a spiritual gift given unto you at that time. Maybe shortly after you received the Holy Spirit, you prayed for somebody and they were healed. Maybe you had a dream and it came to pass. Maybe you had a vision or a word burning in you for somebody and you could find no relief until you were able to deliver that word.

Take a moment and think back. What type of spiritual encounter did your ministering spirit perform through you?

Angels are appointed by the Holy Spirit to minister in accordance with the spiritual gifts that have been imparted to you. For you see, the angels are the ones who are doing the ministering for you. It is not your own willfulness or power that overcomes the natural so that you can walk in the supernatural. It is the angel of the Lord who was sent to do the work for you.

What about Angels?

"You did not despise or reject, but you received me as an Angel of God, even as Christ Jesus. What then was the blessing you enjoyed? For I bear you witness that, if possible, you would have plucked out your own eyes and given them to me" (Gal. 4:14b–15).

Many have despised me for teaching on angels, and yet the Bible is full of the saints of God having multiple encounters with His Angelic Host. Truth will either set you free or convict you. It is obvious that many have been thoroughly convicted by the fact that angels from God are here to help us during these troubling times. The repudiation that we have received from those who judge us and warn others to stay away from us is very much appreciated. Seriously! As the late Kenneth (Papa) Hagin once said, "Negative advertising is the best advertising." With each slanderous comment posted on Facebook, we gain hundreds of seekers of truth.

For many years now, we have seen a continual increase in the presence of angels from God. Now we need to understand why our Heavenly Father is sending His angelic host to us and what we are to expect from this wonderful encounter.

Angels & Impartations of Gifts

As many of you well know, I have been sending out prophesies since 1989. What you may not have known is that He has been giving me prophetic words of impartation appointing His angels to various people, sometimes for multiple purposes. Last year, our Lord began giving me prophetic words and imparting spiritual gifts to those who are ready to receive. This does not mean that if you receive one of these prophecies that everything in your world will immediately change. However, it does mean that you will begin experiencing the nudging to do and say things you would normally not.

Based on which gift the Holy Spirit has given you, it will set the standard for how God is going to use you in the things of the supernatural. For example, if you have been given the gift of faith (I am not talking about what you believe, but rather the power to believe in things you did not even have on your bucket list), the angel appointed to you that ministers in this spiritual gift will drop into your soul and spirit a thought that did not start in your own mind. In other words, this gift of faith is something that happens to you, not something you do just because you want to. This angel is at your side all the time, just waiting for the words that line up with what is being said in Heaven to come out of your mouth. As soon as you speak the true word of faith, that angel immediately begins moving things into place so that what you said will come to pass.

Sometimes it will happen and you will be unaware that you spoke on Earth what is being proclaimed in Heaven. It is written in Luke 11:2, "So He said to them, 'When you pray, say: Our Father in Heaven, Hallowed be your name. Your kingdom come. Your will be done on Earth has it is in Heaven.'"

It Was Prophesied

In 1991, Oral Roberts prophesied that many people would begin to have encounters with the Lord's angels in the years to come. Since that time, there have been a number of documentaries in which common people have testified about their experiences with angels. A weekly television series called *Touched by an Angel* as created in this same decade and has been viewed by millions. There have been virtually hundreds of editorials, books, and devotionals written, even calendars printed, which give witness to the presence of angels in our midst.

There is biblical evidence that angels can also create mass destruction. Sodom and Gomorra were consumed by fire, but it was not an ordinary fire. God's wrath manifested by His angels annihilated these two cities. Today, archeologists are still trying to locate the exact location where these sinful cities once flourished.

Elisha and his servant witnessed the presence of angels when they were surrounded by their enemy, who had come to kill them.

Elisha was not afraid. Why? Because he saw thousands of angels standing behind his enemy, ready to protect him and his servant in the spirit realm (2 Kings 6:15–18).

The Dividing Line

Worldly people want to hold the commandments of Jesus over our heads, though they themselves do not adhere to the same strict rules. Jesus has commanded us to turn the other cheek when our enemies strike us, bless those who curse us, and pray for our adversaries. It can be very confusing to read what Jesus has commanded and then read the scriptures where the apostles cursed those who hindered them. Many Christians today allow people to heap condemnation on them whenever they try to defend and protect their families, properties, jobs, businesses, or ministries. We need to gain balance and understanding regarding this commandment. The fact is that Jesus does give balance in His word.

Much is said in the Bible about blessing those who curse you and praying for your enemies, but does the Bible tell us how to pray? The letter Apostle Paul wrote to the church at Thessalonica indicates that we can pray, as my wife says, "our bad prayer."

We see in Acts 13 that Paul cursed Elymas the sorcerer with blindness. For a period of time after this, Elymas could not see the light of day. Does this sound like blessing the enemy? We must find the precept of God in this spiritual law in order to understand what Jesus was saying. Was Paul out of order when he called forth blindness upon Elymas? Can we cause blindness to come upon anyone we decide to curse? No!

We cannot curse someone without first receiving the Lord's permission and the authority to do so.

Tabernacle of Angels

There are territorial angels of God as well as spirits of the evil one. The church is a great place to find angels. A pub or bar is a good place to find a demon. There are also countries with a large number of angel or demon inhabitants, depending on their religion.

Have you ever walked into a service and felt power hit you? That was the presence of the Lord's angelic host. Ever been caught up in praise and worship and felt someone touch you, yet when you opened your eyes there was no one there? Maybe you have experienced goosebumps while in praise and worship. All of these events are angelic encounters.

Now that we have all these angelic beings with us, we must ask why they are here. Our Lord Jesus is setting the stage where many of us will find ourselves being the voice of His command-ments to these angels who have massive powers. They will be demonstrating powers that can swing to opposite sides of the pendulum, from healing and delivering those who God chooses to bring fire down from Heaven upon the enemies of the Lord's Church. I know it is difficult to see destruction coming out of the mouth of our loving God. You may have a real problem discerning the difference from the love of God and the wrath of God without thinking one side could only be the devil. I understand that many of us are about to be stretched in our theology, but the truth of the matter can be found throughout the Holy Scriptures.

Two Sides of God

God can love and God can hate. He hates sin and the enemies of the Church. What father would not come to the defense of his children, knowing he had the power to protect them? Here again, allow me to ask this question of those who are shepherds of a portion of God's flock. Do you feel called to stand aside and do nothing if you witness the enemy of God destroying what you have been placed over to protect? Our Lord has empowered you to use His power to do all that you can to protect and preserve the church.

It will not be long before we start seeing many of these appointed angels of God raising the dead on the word of those who have an ear to hear what the Spirit of the Lord is proclaiming from His throne. Others will stand in the midst of a deadly storm and command it to be still by the word of the Lord—and it will. Whatever you can think of as being a miracle, you will soon begin to be a part of the signs and wonders taking place daily across the nation and in other lands.

Maybe you thought that all these years we have been equipping the saints for the work of the ministry and learning to pray, hear, and obey, was all just to bless the church. Well, you would be wrong! We have just begun to see all that He has proclaimed that you and I will do! Because greater works we shall do than these, says He! (John 14:12).

Angels of Our Lord

When Jesus was born in a manger, there was an army raised to find him. Every child two years old or under was to be slaughtered because King Herod heard that a king was born. Herod feared losing his position.

An angel appeared unto Joseph and Mary and warned them to leave Judea because Herod sought the life of their newborn son. They left and stayed away for a number of years. Eventually, an angel appeared to them again and let them know that it was safe to return, for King Herod was dead. This was just the beginning of many encounters with angelic hosts in the ministry of Jesus Christ.

When Jesus stood before those who were to judge him on Earth, Pontius Pilate said to him, "Do you not know that I hold your life in my hands? I can give life or I can take it" (see John 19). Jesus replied that Pilate did not know what he was talking about. Jesus knew He had thousands of angels at His disposal (see Matthew 26:53) and at His word, the angels could have destroyed everything.

When Jesus walked into a city, people came from everywhere to seek Him. Jesus did not have to advertise His presence. People just showed up in the middle of nowhere because the angels of the Lord gathered them. Many times Jesus could not find a place to be alone so that He could seek the will of the Father. These encounters are important to us because they are examples of how our lives should be. We are not to worship or pray to angels, but they are there as ministering spirits to minister for us.

Acts 12 tells the story of when Peter was in prison and the congregation was praying for his safe return. An angel went to the prison and struck Peter to wake him up. The angel told him to get his things, then led him out of prison. Peter came to the house where they were praying for him and knocked on the door. A girl peeped out and saw Peter but did not let him in; instead, she went to tell the others he was there. They replied that it could not be Peter at the door, so it must be his angel. Why would they say such a thing?

There are so many references to angels in the Bible. If you were to look up all of the encounters, you would surely be blessed to know that angels are still here ministering for us. They are making sure that the word of God is fulfilled in your life. It should be an effortless deed to walk in the supernatural! When you believe and understand an appointed angel's purpose is to minister for you, your life begins to flow in the supernatural.

Functions of Angels

When Jesus was arrested in the garden of Gethsemane and taken before Pontius Pilate, He told those present that there were over twelve legions of angels at his disposal. That equates to 12,000 angels. "Or do you think that I cannot now pray to My

Father, and He will provide me with more than twelve legions of angels?" (Matt. 26:53). How many angels do you have? Does it make any difference how many angels are appointed to you? All who are born again have at least one angel appointed to watch over us and report our actions to the Lord.

Different angels have different functions. They are not stamped out of the same mold. Each angel has an appointed assignment. Gabriel was sent to Daniel to give him understanding. He was also sent to give understanding to Zacharias, the father of John the Baptist, and to Mary, the mother of Jesus.

Luke 1:18 says, "Zacharias said to the angel [Gabriel], 'How shall I know this? For I am an old man, and my wife is well advanced in years?'"

Luke 1:30–31 says, "Then the angel [Gabriel] said to her, 'Do not be afraid Mary, for you have found favor with God. And behold, you will conceive in your womb and bring forth a Son, and shall call His name Jesus.'"

The archangel Michael, however, was created to be a warring spirit. Many times Michael was involved in fighting the enemies of God and the enemies of God's people. Satan cannot stand against Michael and his angels. Michael is always victorious!

Daniel 12:1 says, "At that time Michael shall stand up, the great prince who stands watch over the sons of your people; and there shall be a time of trouble, such as never was since there was a nation, even to that time. And at that time your people shall be delivered, everyone who is found written in the book."

Jude 1:9 says, "Yet Michael the archangel, in contending with the devil, when he disputed about the body of Moses, dared not bring against him a reviling accusation, but said, 'The Lord rebuke you!'"

Revelation 12:7–8 says, "And war broke out in Heaven: Michael and his angels fought with the dragon; and the dragon and his angels fought, but they did not prevail, nor was a place found for them in Heaven any longer."

Michael and Gabriel are the only two angels mentioned by name throughout the Bible; however, their functions are quite different. In fact, in the book of Daniel, it is said that Michael comes to Gabriel's aid when Gabriel is unable to fight his way through the demonic principalities of the air (Dan. 10:13). It is obvious that angels have different powers. They are not all equal; they receive various measures of power and favor from God.

Angelic Possession

You will find very few Spirit-filled Christians who disagree that a person can be possessed by a demon. If Satan has possession of a person's spirit, soul, and body, he can use that person to fulfill his evil deeds.

From time to time, we see a convict on television confess that the devil took full control over his mind and body. He may say, "I did not know what I was doing." Now, the jury of the world is still out on whether or not this can happen; however, you and I know it can happen, and it has happened far too many times.

Identifying the works of the devil is easy, and those works are reported daily in the news media. It is acceptable for us to say, "Yes, a person can be demon-possessed." However, many refuse to believe an angel can possess a person. Why is this? Both angels and demons are spiritual beings directed by two separate forces: the Holy Spirit or Satan. The possessor of one's spirit will determine who has eternal rights over the person's body, soul, and spirit.

Supernatural events recorded over many centuries have told us how possessed people have accomplished phenomenal feats. Some have been demon-possessed; others possessed by an angel. You may not like to look at it this way, but where there is negative, there is also always positive. It is easy to see that a person committing evil is demon-possessed.

If God needed me to perform a miracle, like flip over a burning bus full of school children, and He wanted an angel to take possession of my body to get the work done, I would not have a problem with that—I don't think you would, either. However, you probably would not agree with me if I were to say that God could possess me with an angel anytime He desires. In fact, there have been many times that I have been prophesying and all of sudden my thoughts are no longer my thoughts, nor my words my own. My mouth was moving, but what was coming out of me was not in my power or ability to even think.

We have also seen supernatural signs follow God's people, but why do we not say they are possessed by an angel? It stands to reason that if Satan is going to work through one of his people, he will appoint a demon—or demons—to fulfill his evil through that person.

Think of it this way: when we operate in the gift of discernment and cast out demons, we are, in effect, casting out evil spirits. You cannot find one scripture in the Bible where Satan is cast out of anyone, because he does not allow himself to be put in that position when he has fallen angels (demons) to do it for him. You will find many accounts in the Bible where demons are cast out of people. The only place Satan has been cast out of is Heaven (Luke 10:18). Remember, demons are simply fallen angels. One third of the angels followed Satan, so two-thirds are still on our side. Think about it; we outnumber Satan 2 to 1.

While We Are in God's Presence

When we witness the power of miracles, we are seeing the work of God's ministering spirits orchestrated by the Holy Spirit. There have been many times that the presence of God was so strong I could see His angels ministering in the midst of the congregation. Next time you are in a service where the gifts of the Holy Spirit are in operation, ask the Lord to open your eyes so that you may see His angels at work. Anytime you see a minister moving in the gifts of the Holy Spirit, you are witnessing someone who is being possessed (spurred, moved by a strong feeling, or under supernatural power) by an angel of the Lord.

"But to which of the angels has He ever said: 'Sit at My right hand, till I make your enemies your footstool'? Are they not all ministering spirits sent forth to minister FOR those who will inherit salvation?" (Heb. 1:13–14).

Acts 10:34–35 says, "Then Peter opened his mouth and said, 'In truth I perceive that God shows no partiality. But in every nation, whoever fears Him and works righteousness is accepted by Him.'" You may be more familiar with the King James Version, "God is no respecter of persons. . ." meaning He shows no favor over one nation, but favors those who do His work of righteousness. Righteousness simply means to be right with God. The only way you can be right with God is to do what God asks of you.

I have heard people quote this scripture, inferring that we are all equal in the eyes of God and that He endows no one more than the other. The fact is that we will *not* be equal in Heaven any more than we are equal here on Earth. Most people have it in their heads that when we go to Heaven we will all be equal, but the decisions we make in this life can modify our eternal life.

Because of what Jesus did for us, we are no longer automatically blessed of God because of our nationality (Gal. 3:26–28). The blessings of God are given as He so wills. In the Old Testament, His choice for king was David because he was a man after God's own heart (1 Sam. 13:14). God was looking for someone who would want to please Him by doing His will. It is still the same today. The Holy Spirit is searching for yielded vessels that will do what He asks of them.

I have learned this much: if I do what the Spirit tells me, then He will respond in the same measure when I ask something of Him. If the Spirit is not answering your prayers, then you are probably not doing all of what He has asked of you.

What we do in this life will determine where we sit with the Lord in His kingdom for eternity. I don't know about you, but I will not be satisfied with simply sweeping Heaven's streets of gold or polishing His pearly gates. The measure you serve God in this life will determine the measure of your reward for eternity.

"So Jesus answered and said, 'Assuredly I say to you, there is no one who has left house or brothers or sisters or father or mother or wife or children or lands, for My sake and the gospel's, who shall not receive a hundredfold now in this time . . . and in the age to come, eternal life'" (Mark 10:29–30).

"For the Son of Man will come in the glory of His Father with His angels, and then He will reward each according to his works" (Matt. 16:27).

There is good reason to serve Christ daily, for in doing so you will receive a greater reward. We obey God because of our love and fear of Him, and for the rewards He gives in this life and in the life to come.

Immanuel, God is with Us

There is no one in history that has been given more names or titles than Jesus Christ. If you've read through the Bible carefully, then you know what I mean. Throughout it, there are over 100 names and titles given to Jesus. Whether He is called Bright Morning Star, Wonderful Counselor, the Root of Jesse, the Alpha and the Omega, or the Lamb of God, each of these names and titles is rich with meaning. They all say something significant about who Jesus is.

However, there is no name more significant than "Immanuel." This name, which Matthew refers to in his Gospel (see Matthew 1:23), was first given to Jesus by the prophet Isaiah 700 years before His birth (Isa. 7:14). This very special Christmas name, as Matthew tells us, means "God with us." Jesus Christ is Immanuel, "God with us," and I'd like to share why this is so meaningful at Christmas time.

When Paul preached to the pagans of Lystra (Acts 14), he reminded them that the true God, the Creator, had always been with them. He had always given them witness of Himself by providing them with rains, fruitful seasons, and giving them food and glad hearts. Thus, God has always been with His creation in the sense that He, who is everywhere, has showered all mankind with blessings—despite their sins.

So great was His love for His fallen creation, for you and me, that He left His glory to come here. Through His perfect life and death on the cross, He broke down the wall of separation that our sins had built and reconciled us to Himself. As it is written, "God was in Christ, reconciling the world to Himself, not imputing their trespasses to them, and has committed to us the word of reconciliation" (2 Cor. 5:19). Through Jesus Christ, Immanuel, our sins are forgiven and we have fellowship with our Creator again.

In this one person, Immanuel, everything humankind needs and the entire plan of God's salvation is culminated. How blessed we are that Jesus Christ became Immanuel, God with us! Even to this day, He is molding and shaping His people through a process I will try to depict through this short analogy, "The Potter's Hands."

The Potter's Hands

This little story somewhat explains the process of being shaped and molded by the Potter's hands. Each of us is nothing more than a clay vessel cleansed of its impurities. God chooses unworthy and broken vessels of clay for His work.

Pausing, the Potter picks up an abandoned and broken vessel of clay. His compassion melts the vessel, forming a new, pliable clay. His newfound love for it begins to knead out the lumpy, hard features of its coarseness.

Finally, the clay sighs in relief as it is gently placed in the center of the Potter's view. The Master ponders what He will make of this reborn vessel. Suddenly, the clay experiences a troubling intrusion. Spinning the wooden wheel, the Master begins to form the clay into His heart's delight, but as the clay feels the strong touch of the Master's hands, he also experiences the swirling of circumstances that he cannot control. Faster and faster, the Potter's wheel turns as He squeezes and shapes the clay, extending its faith and stature. Slowing the wheel, life's problems seem to cease. The Potter sits back and observes His renewed vessel. Noticing a few weaknesses in the vessel, He compresses the clay once again into a shapeless form. The wheel spins around even faster than before, causing confusion in the clay.

As the Potter works the clay, it rises higher and higher. Each finger of the Potter's hand carves deep into the clay, creating deep paths of purpose and destiny. At last, the wheel comes to a halt and the Potter walks away. Standing all alone, the clay begins to cry out for the Master. To his surprise, the Potter returns with a sharp, double-edge sword. "What could He possibly want to do with that?" stuttered the vessel. With one clean stroke of the sword of His word, the clay vessel is freed from the wheel of calamity and confusion. Resting in the hands of its Master, the vessel experiences a great peace as he is handled delicately for a season.

Placed in a small box, the vessel witnesses the closing of a door that only the Master can open. With great intensity, a fire breathes its fury all around the clay vessel. Sweating with fear, the vessel struggles to find faith in the midst of this seemingly cruel process. With every hour seeming like years, the vessel weeps every ounce of moisture from its being. Having no more strength of its own, the vessel begins to harden in the Refiner's fire. As the vessel sees a new glow from his Master's flaming eyes, the vessel recalls its purpose for being created. It recalls the promise of the Potter's return, and the vessel begins to reflect.

Yearning for deliverance, the smoking vessel cries out with a burning desire to serve His creator. As the Potter begins to remove the vessel from the furnace, the vessel vows to serve the Master with every part of his being. Still glowing with passion to tell others about the Potter, the vessel pleads to be used for the Master's glory. Instead, the Potter places the vessel on a cold shelf, knowing that he could scorch another with his heated passion to share his experience. The vessel laments over this chilling experience, waiting impatiently to be called into the service of his Master.

With each new day, the once fiery zeal of the vessel draws cold. Discovering the vessel is cool to the touch and cannot harm those who handle it, the Master takes him from the shelf. Knowing he is called to serve the Master, the vessel waits patiently for the anointed brush of the Potter. With each unique and personal stroke of the Master's brush, the vessel is gifted with a colorful destiny unlike any other. The vessel is complete, ready to be filled with the Master's glory. It is willing to be filled and emptied again and again, delivering hope to those who thirst for the Master's touch.

"But now, O LORD, you are our Father; we are the clay, and you our potter; and we are all the work of your hand" (Isa. 64:8).

Chapter 2

Angels Appointed to Serve You

The Gifts of the Holy Spirit and Angels

While the Lord was teaching me about the laying on of hands and prophecy to receive gifts, He also began to lead me to the scriptures about angels. For more than nine months, I would pray for understanding as I studied the Bible. There are many interesting stories in the Bible about angelic encounters and how angels are used in Heaven and on Earth, but as I studied, I did not put together the two things God had taught me about the gifts of the Holy Spirit and angels. Finally, I began to see a parallel in prophecy and angels through the words in the following verses of scripture.

"Bless the Lord, you His angels, who excel in strength, WHO DO HIS WORD, heeding the voice of His word. Bless the Lord, all you His hosts, you ministers of His, who do His pleasure. Bless the Lord, all His works, in all places of His dominion. Bless the Lord, O my soul!" (Ps. 103:20–22).

These verses spoke volumes of knowledge to me regarding prophecy. Now I know that whatever I see or hear in my spirit from the Lord in Heaven will be done on Earth by His angels. If I can find the Lord in prayer, clearly understand what His will is, and then prophesy His will, the angels will see to it that His word is fulfilled (Luke 11:2). This may not seem like much to you, but it is if you want to see the Lord's will done on Earth as it is in Heaven. This revelation is the key to unlocking the blessings stored up above for those who have an ear to hear.

"And I will give you the keys of the kingdom of Heaven, and whatever you bind on Earth will be bound in Heaven, and whatever you loose on Earth will be loosed in Heaven" (Matt. 16:19).

The Lord has always searched for those who are yielded vessels for Him to speak through. If you speak on Earth His word from Heaven, His angels will see that His Word is manifested.

Once I gained a better understanding of how angels assist in seeing God's will done on Earth through prophecy, I felt more secure, but I still had a question: how do I hear more from the Lord now than before I had the prophet lay hands on me to impart to me this gift I was now walking in? What had happened to me and who could explain the difference in me before and after this event?

Some ministers I asked these questions to told me the reason was that I just began to have more faith that I could hear God.

Others said it was not God speaking at all, because they had never heard Him speak this way.

The answer I had been looking for came as I was reading from the book of Hebrews. One little three-letter word in this verse below stood up and shouted at me. It gave me greater understanding of why I could now hear from the Lord anytime for myself or anyone else.

"But to which of the angels has He ever said: 'Sit at My right hand, till I make your enemies your footstool?' Are they not all ministering spirits sent forth to minister FOR those who will inherit salvation?" (Heb. 1:13–14).

Revelation Has Come

That was it! I had finally been given the understanding. An angel had been appointed to give me the words to speak. This is why I was hearing volumes of information when I would begin to pray. The angel that was given to me also accompanied the gift that was given to me by the Holy Spirit through the hands of the established prophet.

We know that the Holy Spirit is the only one who can give a spiritual gift. No prophet can give gifts as he so wills, but he can give the word and impart the gift that the Holy Spirit has commissioned him to pronounce. In that moment, it all made sense to me.

Always before, when I was preaching, I felt as though I was waiting for a change in the spiritual atmosphere. As soon as I felt the presence of a supernatural power in the room, I would receive instruction in my spirit to pray for someone who was sick or afflicted in his or her body. A different anointing set in as I ministered the word of knowledge.

I have also found that the word of wisdom works more frequently when ministering in prophetic counseling. It is a little like the spirit of prophecy; however, there is not the unalterable will of God in a word of wisdom like there is in prophecy. The ministering angel brings forth the word of wisdom, simply foretelling of what can be expected if the person to whom you are ministering goes another way. The information given is to reveal what they can expect to happen, although what they do will be their decision.

On the other hand, if God sends the spirit of prophecy, that word will come to pass in most cases. However, for both prophecies and words of wisdom, if they are not interpreted correctly then the minister will be considered a fake. I have said for years: "It's not enough to hear God; you must know what He means." Our Lord still speaks words that are difficult to understand. Therefore, if what is heard is not translated correctly, it will appear as if you did not hear God at all.

"Surely the Lord GOD does nothing, unless He reveals His secret to His servants the prophets" (Amos 3:7).

Angels Will Deliver Us:

With so many people smothered in debt, we must be open to receive our deliverance in whatever way He so wills. To reject the vessel He sends to deliver you is to judge the Master. You are falsely adhering to the idea that you somehow know more than God.

A number of years ago, I was ministering in Nacogdoches, Texas. An older lady came up to me during the services in desperate need of help. She said that the bank was going to foreclose on her home. They told her that if she would come into the bank and sign a deed in lieu of foreclosure, she would not be liable for the balance of the loan if the house did not sell for enough money to pay it off. She asked me to help her know what she should do. As I prayed for her, our Father told me to tell her that an angel would go into the bank and destroy all the documents so that she would not lose her home.

A year later, I was back in Nacogdoches, and as I was closing out the meeting, that same lady came up and took the microphone out of my hand. She began to testify that after I had prophesied to her, she reluctantly went to the bank and met with the banker who was to have her sign the papers. As he went to get the papers, she waited in his office. She waited and waited. Finally, the banker apologetically returned and told her that she would have to come back because her file could not be found.

She then told us that months later she received a letter from the bank stating that they would not be foreclosing and that she owed no more money on her house. They also said that they were, regrettably, unable to send her the paid note and mortgage, but that letter would suffice as evidence that the house was paid in full. She shouted, "God's angel destroyed the file!" Over and over she shouted. Amen!

"But at night an angel of the Lord opened the prison doors and brought them out, and said, 'Go, stand in the temple and speak to the people all the words of this life'" (Acts 5:19–20).

Receiving Blessings through Angels

We shall know all things by the Spirit. The things you are in need of cannot always be successfully obtained by human knowledge. That is why God has given us the window of prayer to find answers on how to obtain the things we need. If you are in need of anything, you can find out how to get it through the Spirit. When you pray, God will be faithful in sending to you His ministering spirit to bring the revelation of how you will obtain your needs.

"But seek first the kingdom of God and His righteousness, and all these things shall be added to you" (Matt. 6:33).

One of the recorded events of angels interacting with man is that of Jacob's ladder. It is a Sunday school teaching many of us have forgotten. This recorded event is biblical proof that angels move between Heaven and Earth.

The angels of the Lord are continually ascending and descending between Heaven and Earth, delivering messages from, and delivering prayers to the throne of God. In a dream, Jacob saw angels traveling up and down a ladder that extended from God's throne. The angels were making a way for the word of God to be delivered to Jacob while he slept. The promise of the Lord was given to Jacob during this dream and Jacob knew when he awoke that God had revealed Himself (see Genesis 28:10–16).

The New Testament gives confirmation that a similar occurrence took place during the days Jesus ministered on Earth. While Jesus was ministering in the word of knowledge, He gave the gift of discernment to Nathanael (1 Cor. 12:10).

Philip found Nathanael and told him about Jesus, whom Philip claimed was the Messiah. Nathanael did not believe that Jesus was the Messiah who was prophesied about in the Old Testament. When Jesus saw Nathanael, He spoke a word of knowledge to Nathanael, telling him He had seen him sitting under a fig tree. Nathanael knew there was no way that Jesus could have seen him sitting under the fig tree, thus Nathanael believed that Jesus was the Son of God (see John 1:47–51).

"Jesus answered and said to him [Nathanael], 'Most assuredly, I say to you, hereafter you shall see Heaven open, and the angels of God ascending and descending upon the Son of Man'" (John 1:51).

After Nathanael had publicly recognized Jesus as being the Son of God, the Lord gave him spiritual eyes to see how Jesus knew and operated in these supernatural gifts by giving him the gift of discerning of spirits.

"This Very Day Things Will Change"

In 1995, we were asked to go on television by a friend who worked at LeSea Broadcasting. This individual and his wife became friends of ours after they traveled from Hawaii to Fort Worth, Texas, to meet with me and my wife Andrea, who has since passed away, to receive a word from the Lord. While we ate dinner in a crowded restaurant, he and his wife began to tell us about all of their problems. They were destitute; they had lost everything and did not know where to go or what to do. I had brought a small tape recorder and a blank tape to record their prophecy. It was not long before I received the message the Lord had for this man and his wife.

The spirit told me to tell them to go back to Hawaii. There would be someone there to meet them who would give them a place to live. This portion of the word was not too difficult to believe, but the next part was. He was also to go on Christian television and begin to pray for people over the air.

He and his wife flew home to Hawaii shortly after our visit. Just as God had said, they were met at the airport by a friend and were given a place to live rent free. The second part of the prophecy was fulfilled within weeks of their returning home. This man had no money; however, he was still able to start a TV program, which was to be aired weekly. Within the first few months he was unable to pay the expenses for his program and went off the air. Stressed out, he sent in his last $50 for a prophecy tape and waited for his word.

The word he received was, "This very day things will change." The day he received his prophecy, he also received a phone call from the television station. The station asked if he would start up his program again, but this time as a paid employee of the station so that his television program would not cost him anything. What a blessing it was for this family in Hawaii!

I have shared this story in order to set the stage on how the Holy Spirit took us through an awesome spiritual journey. Becoming friends with this television minister became a wonderful blessing. Eventually, he asked if I would produce a program to be aired on LeSea's network of television stations.

We started our program the first part of 1996 with teachings and prophecies to the viewers. Within a few months, they asked if I would sign a contract placing our program on all eight stations, as well as the satellite LeSea owned. I called PMT's trustees to conduct a meeting regarding this request of LeSea. The board of trustees talked about the lack of funds and discussed whether we could afford to air a television program. We all agreed this was not a good time to accept LeSea's offer.

Just before we were to take a vote, Andrea spoke up and said the Spirit had told her we were to go on all of LeSea's stations. Now, you have to have known Andrea to know how remarkable this was. She was a very conservative woman and did not take many risks. However, if she heard the voice of God say to do something, she would not hesitate to do it. All of us in the meeting knew that she had just heard God. Our planning and guessing would not give us the answer we needed to know what God wanted us to do in this situation.

The Lord had sent His messenger just in time and we gave LeSea our answer that day. I immediately called my minister friend in Hawaii who worked for the station and told him we would go on all 8 stations plus the satellite programming.

Our Lord truly is blessing His people with His angels, making the way for His word to come to pass for those who believe.

Angels as God's Messengers

Many brand name preachers have turned to humanistic teachings when it comes to the supernatural. They attempt to explain away the spiritual gifts through their teaching, saying that the works of Christ Jesus are not for today.

A book by a well-known preacher (whose name I will not reveal) teaches that Jacob's self-will gave him the power to change the color and markings of his father-in-law Laban's goats (See Genesis 30:29–43). This made Jacob's flock larger than Laban's, therefore, Jacob obtained greater riches and wealth, giving him power over his father-in-law. This humanistic teaching goes on to say that Jacob envisioned, or meditated, into existence the speckled and striped goats marked for his flock.

The truth is that while Jacob was sleeping, an angel came to him and gave him the revelation that the crossbred goats, speckled and striped, would increase in number. Jacob made a wager with Laban that every speckled and striped goat would be added to his flock. This is how Jacob obtained the larger flock, by the word of the Lord given through an angel in a dream (See Genesis 31:1–16). Even to this day, it is well-known in the ranching industry that crossbred animals produce healthier and more numerous offspring, as were Jacob's flock.

The will of every person is to be in control of his or her surroundings and future. We are commanded, however, to die to the man within us and allow the Spirit of God to guide us into the unknown. It takes true faith in God to allow the Holy Spirit, who we cannot see, to lead us in the direction God desires for our destiny. If we follow the flesh, we will not experience the awesome adventures and blessings God has for us.

It is very easy to overlook the obvious truth found in the scriptures when a dynamic orator spins his teachings into his own philosophy. I do not mean to be critical of others and their teaching; however, we need not stray from the truths recorded in the Bible.

I do believe the Holy Spirit and the angels of God minister to us and FOR us. There is a difference in hearing the Holy Spirit and hearing an angel of the Lord. First of all, the Holy Spirit is part of the Godhead. An angel is a messenger from the throne of God. It is very clear when the Holy Spirit is speaking, but it is a little fuzzy when an angel speaks. When the Holy Spirit speaks it sounds so clear that you may think you heard Him audibly. When receiving a message from an angel of God, it is like what Apostle Paul said, "Like looking through a glass dimly" (See 1 Corinthians 13:12). Either way, if you are sure of your source, then obey and you will not go wrong.

Dark Angels

Years ago, Andrea related to me an experience she had as a young adult at her home church in Savannah, Georgia. A visiting minister asked the pastor of the church if he could pray for him. When the minister touched the pastor, the pastor fell out under the power of the ministering spirit, the angel.

Andrea saw in the spirit realm a dark form rise up and hover over the body of the pastor as he lay on the floor of the sanctuary. She immediately began to rebuke it, believing that because it was a dark form, it had to be evil. As soon as she began rebuking it, the Lord said, "What are you doing?" She replied, "I am casting out that demon." Then the Lord informed her that it was not a demon, but rather an angel. He went on to explain that it was His warring angel, appointed to watch over the pastor of that church.

Puzzled, Andrea began to pray to the Lord for understanding. She found her confirmation while reading a book by Kenneth Hagin. In the book, Papa Hagin referred to black angels as warring angels. The book indicated that he had met many people through the years who had given similar eyewitness accounts of visitations of warring angels. It just goes to show that you cannot judge a book by its cover or an angel by its form.

Why is God Sending out Angels for Us?

There is a reason God is sending out His angels to minister for us. It is not enough to hear the Voice of God, you need to know what He means and what His purpose is for what He is telling you to do. There are also times you just need to go when He says to go, even if you do not know where or why; you will find out later.

I saw that He started having me prophesy over people He sent my way. Believe me, He is sending hundreds of people. My desk is piled high with requests for personal prophecies! Folks are writing in with hopes that they will have an angel appointed to minister for them. I am not too sure how long God will keep this window open for me to dispatch His appointed angels to minister for His chosen. Therefore, if you feel compelled in any way that He has an angel for you, do not wait because I can only impart these gifts as He makes the way, according to 1 Timothy 4:14.

Now, here is the reason God is sending out His angels. We all know that the economy is a wreck, and not only in our country but around the world as well. It is also obvious that our medical situation is in shambles. The possibilities of recovery from these two areas alone appear to be hopelessly lost. Fear is running rampant throughout the world. Most of us are doing our best to ignore all these negative problems. The point I want to make here is that we will not have to worry about anything, for God is sending His angels to minister for us in healing and prosperity. Those who have an angel appointed to minister for them will be the vessels He will use to do the works that He once did and more, according to His promise found in John 14:12.

Now can you see what God is preparing His people for? I will keep preaching, teaching, and writing about the topic of angels as long as the gifts are being sent out by the Holy Spirit. There are two more messages that I will write, preach, and teach on that I know of; after that, He will probably move me on to another purpose. So please, saints of God, do not miss out on this wonderful blessing from our mighty God.

Know Your Calling

During the month of January 2012, our Lord instructed me to begin commissioning various people into the ministry. Now, this is not the same thing as imparting spiritual gifts according to 1 Timothy 4:14, which reads, "Do not neglect the gift that is in you, which was given to you by prophecy with the laying on of the hands of the Eldership." However, the spiritual gifts do work hand-in-hand with this purpose, for the gift will establish them according to Romans 1:11. "For I long to see you, that I may impart to you some spiritual gift, so that you may be established."

Therefore, as I began to follow our Lord's instruction, He sent various people my way who were called into the ministry. I would sit with them in my study with a microphone and recorder, and I would begin speaking His words into their life.

The amazing thing about commissioning is that His words not only describe what their ministry is about and what they will accomplish, but it also supernaturally opens up a portal from Heaven. This portal allows the ministering spirits to ascend and descend upon the person, delivering their prayers to the throne and returning with God's message and power to do whatever He so desires. This is according to Hebrews 1:14, which poses the question, "Are they not all ministering spirits sent forth to minister FOR those who will inherit salvation?"

What Has God Called You to Do?

Many people have some idea of what their ministry is about. They are drawn to ministries that inhabit a kindred spirit operating in the same type of ministry that they yearn to flow in, but they cannot seem to get started for lack of direction. However, when a person is called, commissioned, and equipped with at least one spiritual gift, they cannot fail. The security of being called commissioned and equipped is like a three-strand cord: it is very difficult to break. The Bible states in Ecclesiastes 4:12, "Though one may be overpowered by another, two can withstand him. And a threefold cord is not quickly broken."

All Are Called but Few Are Chosen

I now know the reason why these wandering souls feel left out. They have not been recognized in the body of Christ as one who is called of God. They lack direction because they have not been commissioned and feel powerless because they have not perfected their spiritual gift. Being commissioned is like giving sight to the blind; once you have been commissioned you "know in your knower" where the Lord is taking you, assured your spiritual gift will always be there to back you up in all you proclaim in the mighty name of our Lord, Jesus Christ. "For the gifts and the calling of God are irrevocable" (Rom. 11:29).

PMT Mission Statement

We are building the Prophetic Tabernacle of God one living stone after another. Hundreds of new prophetic ministers are being raised up as the Holy Spirit skillfully directs the leadership of PMT where each chosen vessel fits in the Master's plan. The Holy Spirit has chosen a people who have been kicked to the curb by the very people they tried to serve. By the anointing and resurrection power of Jesus Christ, the Rock of our salvation, we are raising up prophets for the next generation. There are thousands of prophetic people of God being sent our way who are now finding their place in His Kingdom.

The Holy Spirit is empowering this army of believers to march in the fullness of their calling; receiving the impartation of their spiritual gifts through prophecy and the laying on of hands. Commissioned and equipped, these conveyors of The Vision of the Tabernacle are being sent as messengers of His divine plan for building a world-wide Prophetic Church; one living stone after another.

Chapter 3

Miracle-Working Angels of God

Jesus, Our Mentor and Teacher

J esus is not only our Savior and Lord, but also our Mentor and Teacher through His Holy Spirit. He is our King and our example. Even so, when Jesus came to Earth, it took Him three and a half years to show His disciples how to walk in the supernatural with evidence through signs and wonders. While here, Jesus was able to receive the encounter of miraculous interventions. He did many healings and many miracles, in many different ways.

Sometimes Jesus would spit in the dirt, make mud, then place it on a blind man's eyes. It is written that He would even spit directly on the blind eyes. Other times, He would touch the person's tongue. You do not see these same types of ministries today because it is not socially acceptable.

How did Jesus know what to do in order for miracles to manifest? He has shown us how—He prayed to the Father and did whatever the Father told Him to do. It worked 100% of the time.

Angels Bring Healing:

Our government is going through major changes and the economy is souring before our very eyes. We all know of someone who has been exposed to the effects of this bitter root. The need for healing agents will become the cry of the people as our nation's medical system becomes very selective about who will receive care. It is obvious that the Church of the Living God is rapidly being marked as an enemy of the State.

Therefore, our faith in Christ Jesus will either grow or it will turn against Him and everyone who He sends to help. I have been ministered to by angels of God many times and each time I knew in my spirit that Christ Jesus had sent them to heal and set me free.

Jesus our Lord said, "I do only that which I see the Father do." You need eyes to see and ears to hear in order to know what to do for the healing to be effective. When reading the Bible, we find that Jesus sometimes did some odd things. One time He just said, "Go and sin nor more for you have been made whole." Angels ascended and descended upon the Son of Man, bringing the Father's Word for what He was to do each time.

Jesus also said to Peter in Matthew 16:19, "I will give you the keys of the kingdom of Heaven, and whatever you bind on Earth will be bound in Heaven, and whatever you loose on Earth will be loosed in Heaven."

If we are commissioned to go forward and follow the example of our Lord Jesus, we must be willing to accept all that He has because He has given unto us the keys to the Kingdom. His Word is the key for every situation; however, it will only work if you are willing to accept the manner in which He chooses to deliver it to you.

John 5:3–4 records that, "In these lay a great multitude of sick people, blind, lame, paralyzed, waiting for the moving of the water. For an angel went down at a certain time into the pool and stirred up the water; then whoever stepped in first, after the stirring up of the water, was made well of whatever disease he had."

Angels Appointed to Serve You!

Angels are being appointed today and they are being sent forth to minister for you.

"Most assuredly, I say to you, he who believes in me, the works that I do he will do also; and greater works than these he will do, because I go to My Father" (John 14:12).

As our Lord has instructed, many have received an impartation of one or more of the spiritual gifts through His Word being prophesied. These gifts were "given to you by prophecy with the laying on of the hands" (1 Tim. 4:14). Being that I am not always able to physically lay hands upon those who have received their personal prophecy that we've sent by e-mail or CD, our Lord has made some very unusual exceptions to this scripture. For years, people have told me wonderful testimonies of demons being cast out and sicknesses being healed when I have prayed over handkerchiefs and had them mailed out to them.

"Now God worked unusual miracles by the hands of Paul, so that even handkerchiefs or aprons were brought from his body to the sick, and the diseases left them and the evil spirits went out of them" (Acts 19:11–12).

God is having us prophesy over His people, appointing a ministering spirit or angel to minister in a specific spiritual gift for that person whom God has selected. Here is the part that is the most exciting: in most of these prophesies, He is giving the spiritual gifts through the prophecy and commissioning the angel to go to them and lay hands upon them, i.e. imparting the spiritual gift. Now isn't that just out of the park! He is not using a human to impart the gift, but the angel that has been commissioned to minister for that person who received the prophecy in the spiritual gift given by the Holy Spirit. People, we are in for a rockin' awesome move of God!

You are Gifted, whether You Are Aware of it or Not

Today we want to see 100% accuracy in the gifts of the Holy Spirit moving in the Body of Christ. The world needs to see the evidence that Jesus is alive and working through His Body, the

Church. We are each members of the Body of Christ, and each of us has a function and purpose. We all have a gift whether we are aware of it or not. The gift is there, even though it may lay dormant for a long time.

We need to be aware of how Jesus was moved and how He ministered. The things Jesus did were done according to the will of the Father. He said, "I do nothing of my own authority. I speak what I hear the Father say" (see John 8:28). This is the true Christian way. His works while on Earth were demonstrations of what we are to do. We may even perform greater works than He, according to John 14:12.

Many times Jesus would pray to find out what the Father had to say, and when Jesus prayed there were angels ascending and descending upon Him, giving Him instructions from Heaven above. Jesus prayed, "Thy will be done on Earth, as it is in Heaven" (Matt. 6:10). That means we need to find out first from Heaven what needs to be done. When we find out what it is that we are to do, nothing can stop us because the authority of His Word is working through us.

Powers of Angels

The manifestation of the gifts of the Holy Spirit is a sign from God that He is alive and watching over us. You may have never thought of it this way, but I learned this truth from the Holy Spirit.

Angels are ministering for us as we operate in these gifts. When you are slain in the spirit, it can feel like someone physically pushed you down or clipped you behind the knees. This is an angel of the Lord doing the work of the Holy Spirit.

Have you noticed that some ministers demonstrate more of the gifts in their ministry than others? This is because they have more angels appointed to them than other ministers. When you are ministering, you begin to recognize the presence of the various angels. This is one way we know what gift the Holy Spirit will have us operate in next. The presence of the ministering spirit that slays people in the Holy Ghost is different from the ministering spirit, that brings the gift of healings.

There are various gifts and ministry functions imparted by God that are appointed to different people. One of these functions is the gift of healings. Not healing, but *healings*. It is plural.

"And God has appointed these in the church: first apostles, second prophets, third teachers, after that miracles, then gifts of healings, helps, administrations, varieties of tongues" (1 Cor. 12:28).

There are angels that have different powers over disease and sickness, just as Gabriel has different powers than Michael, the Archangel.

I have seen people get frustrated and turn from using the gift God has given them. At times, they would pray for the sick and those people would be healed, while other people would not be healed when they prayed. Out of frustration, they gave it up all together.

We are to perfect the gift by using it until we find out the measure of its power. What power does the ministering spirit have that is appointed to you?

To experience the accuracy of any gift, you must first find your calling. When you know your calling and begin following its course, then you can focus on your gift. Most people want to just move in their gift, but do not have a clue what their calling is. If you do not follow your calling, your angel is not obligated to minister for you, hence no manifestation of the gifts.

Your calling may be evangelism, teaching faith, hearing God, feeding the poor, helping in orphanages, or visiting prisoners. Whatever you are called of God to do, He is faithful to endorse it by signs and wonders following after you. However, if we are not willing to do what God has called us to do then He is not bound to send His angels to minister for us. Once you have clarity of what your calling is, begin moving out on what you know.

When dealing with the prophetic angels are a vital part in seeing the word delivered with power. Angels are sent to signify and clarify what God's purpose is for His people and for the lost.

The book of Revelation was given to John by an angel. Prophets of today cannot deny that prophecy, words of knowledge, and words of wisdom are given to them in part by angels. To deny that His angels are speaking to us today would be to say that the Holy Scriptures are a lie.

"Then he [the angel] said to me, 'These words are faithful and true.' And the Lord God of the holy prophets sent His angel

to show His servants the things which must shortly take place'"
(Rev. 22:6).

God Works in Mysterious Ways

Miracles continue to manifest just as they have been for many years. Things happen all the time; I recall when my weekly routine involved going to the early morning men's prayer breakfast each Friday. As usual, I was the first to show up, and since I had a key to the building I went in and started brewing some coffee. After a couple of cups, I wondered if anyone was going to show up.

I watched the clock tick away for twenty minutes, and still no one had shown. As I waited I caught sight of an 18-wheeler slowly pulling up to the curb. The driver sat in his truck for a minute then lumbered toward the building. I greeted the grizzly-looking man, asked his name and invited him in for a cup of coffee. He had never been to any of our prayer breakfast meetings and didn't know any members of our church.

While we waited for the others to show up, the trucker began to tell me about his life. He was suffering from various addictions and was on the verge of divorce. His father was an alcoholic, as were his brothers, who were always entrenched in arguments with one another.

A short time later a couple of the regular members showed up, and as we prepared to pray for the trucker, the Lord told me to take out my handkerchief and have everyone grab a corner. As we did, the presence of the Holy Spirit filled the room, and in that moment the trucker gave his life to Jesus. When he gave his life over to God, his countenance immediately began to change. I instructed the trucker to take the handkerchief with him and tell his entire family what had happened.

A few months went by. One Sunday morning, as I looked over the congregation, I was surprised to see that once beaten-down soul now dressed in a suit and tie, with his wife and children at his side and a smile on his face. After the sermon he asked if he could testify. The trucker told the congregation that he had taken the handkerchief to his father who was in the hospital dying of heart disease and cirrhosis of the liver from alcohol abuse. In the room with the trucker were his brothers, who also abused alcohol and drugs. As instructed, the trucker took the handkerchief and laid it upon his dying father. Weeping and praying, suddenly his father came out of his coma. Within three days, the father was released from the hospital and taken home. The entire family celebrated their father's miracle and the trucker led his father, brothers, and their families through the sinner's prayer to receive Jesus Christ as their Lord and Savior.

Since that day our Lord Jesus has graciously blessed hundreds of people from sicknesses, diseases, and evil spirits. As of January 27, 2012, our Lord instructed me, according to first Timothy 4:14, to use an anointed handkerchief in place of laying on of my physical hands to impart the spiritual gifts when I prophesy into their lives. The results have been overwhelming, with hundreds of testimonies telling of miraculous encounters and with evidence of the manifestation of these various spiritual gifts working in their lives.

Jesus is not in the Entertainment Business

Many of us fall into the trap of condemning those who do not know or respect our Lord Jesus, but in doing so we miss the blessing and opportunity that our Lord gives us to bring them into His presence.

Jesus wants us to be obedient to His call. If you are where Jesus wants you to be at the right time and the right place, you will see signs and wonders and the unbelievers will believe. Some believers feel we are putting too much emphasis on the gifts of the Holy Spirit and spiritualization. They instruct us to evangelize more than move in the gifts.

Well, this is what Jesus said about signs and wonders: "Unless you people see signs and wonders, you will by no means believe" (John 4:48). Need I say more? Prophetic evangelism is the way our Lord is leading His people during this spiritually hostile age.

"But if all prophesy, and an unbeliever or an uninformed person comes in, he is convinced by all, he is convicted by all. And thus the secrets of his heart are revealed; and so, falling down on his face, he will worship God and report that God is truly among you" (1 Cor. 14:24–25).

Many people want to move in the signs and wonders but do not want to give up their public imagine or be tagged as a spiritual fanatic. They are more concerned about their reputation than being used of God. They want to experience the power of God but are not willing to yield to God. Most everyone I talk to wants to see God move more in the church, but how are we going to do that?

From the pulpits, we have spent far too many years teaching on the miracle-working powers of God without the demonstration. Many words have been given to thousands upon thousands of folks, claiming they have this or that gift, but too many of those people are still waiting for God to start using them. Over the years, a few have stepped out giving their all to God and were able to move into their specialized gifting.

We can only talk about signs and wonders for so long before people stop believing. The people who are lost and lukewarm must see the signs and wonders that we preach and teach about so that they may believe, as scripture says, "For the kingdom of God is not in words but in power" (1 Cor. 4:20).

Jesus Christ is not in the entertainment business. We should not attend church or meetings expecting to be entertained by the Holy Spirit. If you want to see the gifts subside or fade away, then stop bringing the lost to church. Signs and wonders are for the unbelievers to witness so that they may believe as well as receive the help they came expecting. Signs and wonders will stop flowing through a ministry or church if there are only believers in the group.

Many times we are surrounded by those who need Jesus Christ that are not Christians. They need a miracle in their lives. That is the time to allow the signs and wonders of God to flow through you. This is the time when God wants to show His best. You can say to them in faith, "My God will fix your problem if you give Him your life. Do you want to be healed? If not, then go your own way, but if you want my God to heal you then give yourself to Him right now." Then watch and see what God will do! This is what it is all about! Even prophecies, words of knowledge and wisdom, are for this purpose—so that the unbelievers may believe.

When a prophetic word is given, it is for the purpose of knowing that God can speak directly to us. Christ will reveal to you that the prophetic word given is the truth, and the gifts and callings of God are irrevocable.

Find the Vein

There are many who have the gift of healings. "Healings" is plural. Each one has a gift for different healings. One person might be able to pray and remove headaches. Another may have the gift for healing diabetes, but not headaches. Each person needs to find out their particular healing gift. Many get frustrated because of ignorance because we do not understand the mysteries of the Kingdom of Heaven.

There is a "spiritual vein" that you will need to find and flow in before your gift will work. When you preach about hearing

God, they will hear God. If you preach about healing, they will be healed. If you preach about demons, guess what? They will find demons. When you preach or teach what you have been called of God to share your angel will show up to endorse the message by ministering in signs and wonders.

It does not matter how long you have been a Christian. You can be present in the natural but not yet arrived in the spiritual. You do not need to be a biblical scholar to be able to move in the Holy Spirit. Some of the most anointed people are those who cannot read or write. God chooses the foolish. He does not choose the noble or the wise, but the willing and the yielded.

This is what God wants: "For you see your calling, brethren, that not many wise according to the flesh, not many mighty, not many noble are called, but God has chosen the foolish things of the world to put to shame the wise, and God has chosen the weak things of the world to put to shame the things which are mighty" (1 Cor. 1:26–27).

Many people are waiting for God to move in their lives after they finish reading all the books of the Bible. Worshipping your Bible will not get you signs and wonders! Only worshipping the One the Bible is about will get you there. There is so much more to learn about our Lord Jesus. You learn much more by walking and talking with Him daily. You will learn so much more by allowing Him to use you to minister in signs and wonders than reading the testimonies of others who have. I have learned more about our

Lord Jesus by hearing Him for others than I could ever learn from ten thousand sermons and teachings about Him.

We need to be sensitive to the Holy Spirit so that we will know what He wants us to do. We need to have our spiritual antennas up at all times. Like Apostle Paul said, "Pray without ceasing," meaning be in a state of mind to hear His Spirit 24/7/365. The only effective way for this to happen is to turn off the world and turn up the voice of Christ in your life.

It is so easy to listen to the spirit of fear, scripture says to resist the devil and he will flee. Do not listen to the voice of the devil he lies and delivers fear into your life. "Therefore submit to God. Resist the devil and he will flee from you" (James 4:7).

Seek the Lord and ask Him what to do. You will receive revelation on how to get out of the situation, but only if you will humble yourself before Him. There is hope—a lot more than you know. Know who you are in Christ. Get out of your identity crisis and you will find much, much more to this life than retiring after thirty years of service and collecting your pension. Walking with Jesus and allowing Him to use you in signs and wonders is a big part of the abundant life He promised. "The thief does not come except to steal, and to kill, and to destroy. I have come that they may have life, and that they may have it more abundantly" (John 10:10).

Our First Ministry Road Trip

After just a few weeks of being on the radio, the Prophetic Ministries Today program was gaining listeners. During one Saturday morning program, God told me to tell the people that we were busting out of this place, taking His grace. Calls from all over began to flood the radio station, with people asking us to come to their city.

Soon after, we began to hold meetings in our home to train a group of people who had recently discovered they had the gift of prophecy. Before long, we were scheduling meetings, setting up locations, dates, and times. We were ready to make our first weekend road trip. We even sent out a man of God with a powerful gift of intercession before us so that he could beseech our Father to send his angels and prepare the city for our first prophetic meeting.

The day had finally come for us to take our ministry on the road. As we all gathered to leave, we made a circle, held hands, and began to pray for Jesus' anointing. There were about fourteen people ministering, including a blind woman, with whom I was not familiar. This woman came along to pray for us as we all prophesied. The anointing fell upon us as we began to pray in the Spirit. Some who were praying went out under the power, while others went to their knees. It was a powerful beginning to what would be an astounding outpouring of the Spirit!

As we prayed, the Holy Spirit told me to spit in the blind woman's eyes and He would heal them. I thought about it and wondered

how I was going to do this. I had only met the lady just a few minutes ago. I took too long to make up my mind and the opportunity
for her to receive her healing passed. When the meeting ended, I
took the woman by the arm, and as she tapped her red and white
striped cane we carefully walked down the steps toward the cars.

When I knew that she had mastered the rhythm of the steps,
I told her what the Holy Spirit told me during the prayer. She
stopped and shouted, "He told you that and you didn't spit in my
face? What is wrong with you?" She started swinging her cane at
me; she even hit me a few times! I apologized, and she made it
very clear that the next time I should not wait, but do exactly what
He says, no matter what it is.

Chapter 4

God's Bodyguards for the Body of Christ

M any of us forget that demons were angels of the Lord before they followed Satan. God does use evil men at times to bring about His will. He used the Pharaoh of Egypt to drive the children of Israel out of that evil land and into the wilderness. God has mercy and compassion on whomever He chooses. At times He empowers evil people to chasten His own children. My response to those who teach demonology is that they have lost sight of what the Lord commanded us to preach.

We are commissioned to preach Jesus, His crucifixion and the gospel message, but not the works of the devil. We are commanded to simply cast out demons, not to preach about them. Too much credit is being given in the church to Satan's works, rather than being given to God. If you teach about the devil long enough, he will start helping you to glorify his works rather than the works of Christ. Searching for the works of the devil will produce evil and will lead to a critical spirit. For me, I would rather be looking for the angels of the Lord and seeing their miraculous works on behalf of our Lord and Savior, Jesus Christ.

If you are doing what God has called you to do, the devil cannot stop you. The devil is created for three purposes:

1) To tempt, test and punish us.
2) To steal our blessings by getting us to come into agreement with his lies.
3) To be God's rod of affliction, doing His dirty work punishing His offenders.

You may find these next few verses to be eye openers. They can help those who are seeking to know more about God's ways.

"For God said to Moses, 'I will have mercy on whomever I will have mercy, and I will have compassion on whomever I will have compassion.' So then it is not of him who wills, nor of him who runs, but of God who shows mercy. For the Scripture says to Pharaoh, 'For this very purpose I have raised you up, that I might show my power in you, and that my name might be declared in all the earth'" (Rom. 9:15–17).

There is a man I met several years ago. He was from Nicaragua and had gone through a great persecution under the evil hand of his nation's government. In the early 1980s he received Christ as his Lord and Savior and was baptized in water and Spirit. His name is Louis Pena, and many pastors in his homeland know about this testimony that I am about to share with you.

Louis was radically saved and wanted everyone he met to receive Christ. He preached in open-air meetings, churches, even while standing in line for provisions. Wherever he went, he preached Jesus. Not long after his conversion, his country experienced a change in government and preaching Jesus became a crime punishable by death. This new law did not stop Louis; he kept on preaching. He was warned many times not to continue, but he did not stop.

During a closed and secret revival meeting, the State Police raided the services and arrested all of the pastors and Louis. They were taken away, imprisoned, tied to chairs, and beaten. Louis and all of the pastors from the raid where placed in one room and ordered by the police to denounce Christ and never mention His name again.

Louis was the first in line. They placed a pistol to his head and told him that if he did not do as he was ordered, they would shoot him. He refused to denounce Christ, but rather asked God to forgive the policemen, for they did not know what they were doing. After the captain realized that Louis was not going to obey his orders, he commanded the police officer holding the gun to Louis' head to shoot him. In the presence of all of the pastors and the police, the gun went off, but Louis was still sitting in the chair praying in the Spirit.

With the gun placed within inches of Louis' head, the captain ordered the gun to be fired again. Louis still was not harmed. The police captain ordered his officer to hand him the gun. He checked the remaining bullets, returned it to the officer, and ordered him to empty the gun into Louis' head. Obeying the captain, the officer rapidly fired the pistol point blank until it was empty. Louis was still unharmed. The police became very frightened as Louis kept praying to the Lord. White as sheep, the Nicaraguan police untied Louis and the pastors, releasing them to do whatever they pleased.

Now, I might have a problem believing this testimony if I had just heard the story. However, I have read the letter signed by all of the witnessing pastors which attests to the truth of this event. I have also met Louis Pena and know that he is a Man of God and I believe that his story is true.

"The angel of the Lord encamps all around those who fear Him, and delivers them. Oh, taste and see that the LORD is good; blessed is the man who trusts in Him!" (Ps. 34:7–8).

It does not matter what the devil tries. He cannot be successful, if we are in the will of God, for His angels will be with us to protect us in supernatural ways. There is much more to being in the will of God than just finding an event in the Holy Bible that we decide to mimic and then expect God to give us protection.

When tempted by Satan in the wilderness Jesus said, "You shall not tempt the Lord your God." Satan was trying to get Jesus to prove His identity by having Him jump off the pinnacle of the Temple. "Satan told Jesus, 'If You are the Son of God, throw yourself down. For it is written: "He shall give His angels charge over you, and in their hands they shall bear you up, lest you dash your foot against a stone'"" (Matt. 4:6).

Jesus knew that even He could not just pick from the scriptures a verse and command our Father to live up to what He had written. NO! Jesus knew He could only do that which the Father told HIM to DO and could speak with authority only if He heard the Father give Him the word to speak. Too many Christians today are quoting scriptures and commanding God to do something for them, because they have found His promises in the Bible. This is Satan's way of doing things, not the Lord's. Do not tempt the Lord by commanding Him to do what is written in the scriptures.

"Jesus said, 'You search the Scriptures, for in them you think you have eternal life; and these are they which testify of me. But you are not willing to come to me that you may have life'" (John 5:39–40).

I Will Send You Someone to Defend You

In the summer of 1989, I was asked to join The Southwest Conference of Apostles and Prophets to be held in Dallas, Texas. I was new to the ministry and felt so honored to be a part of such a distinguished group of senior ministers. I received a formal invitation in the mail about a month before the conference was to meet and it seemed to take forever for the days to go by.

Finally, the day arrived and I was headed to Dallas, wearing my finest suit and tie for the big event. As I drove happily, I was not really thinking of anything in particular when God said, "Keep your tongue to roof of your mouth and I will send one to defend you." I had no idea what He was talking about or when this commandment was to be initiated, so I kept driving, not giving too much thought to what our Father meant. I wondered if maybe He just did not want me to talk too much at the conference.

The meeting was held at the Doubletree Hotel, north of the Dallas/Fort Worth International Airport. After everyone had located their assigned seating, the meeting began. The meeting was composed of about 40 well-known ministers. It did not take too long before I noticed a number of the men looking my direction, as they leaned over appearing to ask the person next to them who I was. I felt no discomfort, for I was still riding high on the fact that I was in the presence of these powerful men of God.

I soon began to figure out that this was a business meeting of sorts. A discussion began about what action might need to be taken in regards to a certain minister. I, along with a few other men around me, began looking around wondering who they were talking about. Then a few clues began to surface as questions were asked about this minister. I recall one minister from the Boston area stood up in defense of the minister in question. He stated that he knew of a prophet who offered pieces of his t-shirt he had worn while in prayer for an offering. He went on to say that if churches would put these prophets on their payroll, the prophets would not have to do such things in order to keep their ministries alive.

Next, a prophet from Oklahoma stood up and announced that this prophet that was the center of this controversy was sending out prophesies without the oversight of an apostle. Right behind him stood an apostle who began to demand action against this prophet in question because he was prophesying outside of the church. Many other ministers still did not know who they were talking about, although the realization that I could be this unknown prophet began to settle in.

The morning session flew by and then we all moved to a large ball room to have lunch and hear a message from Pastor John Hagee from San Antonio, Texas. There were about 500 ministers from around the world. Only invited ministers were allowed to attend any of the meetings, and after hearing the message from Dr. Hagee I could understand why. He railed upon the ministers by name who he considered to be a disgrace to God and the church, saying things that were not for the ears of the milk-fed Christians.

After we broke up the lunch meeting, where we heard the message from Dr. Hagee, we returned back to the meeting room where we started earlier that morning. To my surprise, the men on both sides of me had moved their seat to another table. It was strange, but I thought maybe they just wanted to sit by people they knew. However, right before the meeting got started one of the ministers came over to my table with tears in his eyes and gave me a scripture that was intended to comfort me. I thought it was rather odd, because I was feeling just fine and could see no reason to be concerned.

As the head minister at the table began to open the meeting up for new business, a man stepped into the room that was not present during the morning meeting. Immediately this man was acknowledged, and many stood up in honor of his presence. As he made his way in, he must have noticed that there were not many chairs available for him. Seeing me with two empty chairs, one on each side of me, he started making his way toward me. As other ministers tried to give him their chair, he would quickly thank them and continue walking my way until he was finally sitting right beside me.

After everything settled down, the head table started the meeting up right where they had left off. It did not take long for everyone in the room, except the minister who had just sat down next to me, to know that I was the prophet whose integrity was being questioned. I found it odd that no one ever addressed me directly. Lists of allegations were formed against me, and many opinions were openly presented for the ministers to consider.

Normally, I would have stood up and given these men a piece of my mind, but I was under such a wonderful covering of God's grace that I just kept smiling at everyone, remembering what He had said to me as I drove to the meeting: "Keep your tongue to the roof of your mouth and I will send one who will defend you."

As the list was read and the meeting opened for more discussion, I noticed that the minister who had sat down next to me stood up. The head table recognized him, and when he opened his mouth it was like a roaring fire was coming out of him. He began to point out that he had been practicing all of my alleged wrong-doings, as well as doing so without the oversight of an apostle. He responded as though they might have been talking about him. The men at the head table immediately went into spin mode as they began to back down from the allegations, assuring him that they were not accusing him.

Then the man, still steaming, said, "I don't know who you are talking about here today, but I would advise you not to go with what you are planning or you will find yourself coming against me and every prophet that is doing the will of God."

Immediately, the meeting moved on to another topic as the man of God leaned over and shook my hand and left the meeting. I was in awe of what had just happened. The man of God was the late Leonard Fox, who was on the forefront of the Latter-Day Rain prophetic movement of the early days. Prophet Leonard Fox ministered alongside the likes of William Branham, A.A. Allen, Jack Cole Sr., and many others who have gone on to be with our Master. Needless to say, I was never again harassed by any of these ministers.

Leonard Fox was a rare gift to the Body of Christ, an excellent expository preacher, a man with a vision for missions and church planting, and a prophetic ministry that touched thousands of lives. We will all miss him profoundly! He was a great spiritual mentor and pastor. Brother Fox was a foundation builder, mentoring many young preachers and helping them find God's way. We honor him as a true father of the faith and a true Prophetic Pastor.

Judging Angels

"And no wonder! For Satan himself transforms himself into an angel of light" (2 Cor. 11:14).

"Now it happened, as we went to prayer, that a certain slave girl possessed with a spirit of divination met us, who brought her masters much profit by fortune-telling. This girl followed Paul and us, and cried out, saying, 'These men are the servants of the Most High God, who proclaim to us the way of salvation.' And this she did for many days. But Paul, greatly annoyed, turned and said to the spirit, 'I command you in the name of Jesus Christ to come out of her.' And he came out that very hour. But when her masters saw that their hope of profit was gone, they seized Paul and Silas and dragged them into the marketplace to the authorities" (Acts 16:16–19).

I think it is safe to say that this slave girl was possessed by a demon. Even though she wasn't saying anything bad about Apostle Paul and Prophet Silas, she was annoying them as she was being controlled by a demonic spirit. Yet Apostle Paul had the power to cast the demon out of her, which he did, leaving her powerless:

Now when they had gone through the island
to Paphos, they found a certain sorcerer, a false

prophet, a Jew whose name was Bar-Jesus, who was with the proconsul, Sergius Paulus, an intelligent man. This man called for Barnabas and Saul and sought to hear the word of God. But Elymas the sorcerer (for so his name is translated) withstood them, seeking to turn the proconsul away from the faith. Then Saul, who also is called Paul, filled with the Holy Spirit, looked intently at him and said, 'O full of all deceit and all fraud, you son of the devil, you enemy of all righteousness, will you not cease perverting the straight ways of the Lord? And now, indeed, the hand of the Lord is upon you, and you shall be blind, not seeing the sun for a time.' And immediately a dark mist fell on him and he went around seeking someone to lead him by the hand. Then the proconsul believed, when he saw what had been done, being astonished at the teaching of the Lord (Acts 13:6–12).

Here we find scripture that challenges mainstream doctrine, for we see that Apostle Paul performed a work of the Lord by blinding a man. You may be thinking, "Now hold up just a minute! I thought that the devil would only put blindness and sickness on us, but not the Lord. What kind of ministry is this anyway?" There is also a place we find in the Holy Bible where an angel of God put worms in a man that ate him to death. (See Acts 12:20–24)

Something isn't right, and it has to be the teaching that we have been fed over the years. We know that the written word of God is infallible, right?

My point is that we can no longer judge things by what we have been taught. We must be able to discern what is of God by the Spirit, not by our personal or denominational doctrines. If we believe that the Holy Bible is the inerrant word of God, then we must read it and allow the anointing to teach us, and not go on man's theories alone.

"But the anointing which you have received from Him abides in you, and you do not need that anyone teach you; but as the same anointing teaches you concerning all things, and is true, and is not a lie, and just as it has taught you, you will abide in Him" (1 John 2:27).

There will be many scriptures along the way that we will cover that stand against a number of today's doctrinal views that need to be corrected. In other words, apologies are in order. We know that God is a God of Love and that His Love is the most excellent gift, according to 1 Corinthians 13. However, this does not mean that God will allow His Word to be discarded. For example, there are Christians who are teaching that there is no Hell and that God would never allow harm to come upon us. They are teaching that it is okay for God's values to be discarded because, after all, He is a God of Love. "He cannot punish you. Do whatever you want because He won't harm you," they say.

What kind of demon is this, whispering in the ear of these teachers of iniquity? The Bible, specifically Hebrews 12, reveals that God chastens those whom He loves and the ones He does not punish are not His.

Another very clear thing that I read in the Holy Scriptures is that we are to fear God, and anyone who comes after His children or tries to take God's position or discard His values, He will destroy.

There is a reason why our God is sending out His angels at this present time. We are about to witness the manifestation of what His angels can do for those who are willing to turn from their own opinions and start living according to His Word.

God's angels are being sent forth to deliver His defense, His healings, and His miracles to His people. In many places in the Holy Scriptures, we read that He sent His Word, and His angels wiped out entire nations. He is the same God as yesterday and has not changed. Unfortunately, the Church and our nation have drastically changed. At this point in time, history is about to be made. His Word will be sent, and when spoken on Earth as it has been spoken in Heaven, everything will change and it will make straight the way of the Lord.

An Encounter between Peter and Simon Magus

There is an encounter which Peter had that is not recorded in the Bible. We do not know the truth of this event, but I thought I would pass on this record of history to you.

Peter was in Rome to refute the apparent miracles of a false messiah, Simon Magus. As a massive crowd awaited the outcome, Simon, who had won the initial skirmishes, was now pushed to the brink and boasted he would prove his divinity by flying "up unto God." Leaping from a wooden tower, the Magus [magician] aided either by magic spells or by demons, sailed across the sky, seemingly victorious. The crowd looked to Peter for his reaction.

The Apostle implored the Lord Jesus to have Simon "fall from the height and be disabled; and let him not die but . . . break his leg in three places." The impostor plummeted to the ground. He was carried off, his leg broken in three places, at last humiliated. This tale, from the apocryphal Acts of Peter, is one of many Simon Magus stories ("After Jesus," Readers Digest).

"Jesus Christ is the same yesterday, today, and forever" (Heb. 13:8).

Today, we still have the power to call upon the name of Jesus when His glory is being tested by the false prophets. The psychics are today's false prophets.

Testing the Spirits

In 1995, I had the privilege of going to Hawaii to minister for three weeks. During my stay, I was asked to be interviewed on two television programs. In the last twenty minutes of the first program, the station opened up the phone lines for viewers to call in for personal prophecy. The station manager was shocked when, within a twenty-minute span, 78 viewers were waiting on the lines for their word.

The next day, the manager had me come back and wanted to give more time for people to call. With eleven telephones manned in the station, we answered 256 phone calls in forty-two minutes. It was obvious that the people in Hawaii were hungry for spiritual direction.

Being new to Hawaii, I did not know that the islands were also a mecca for the psychics. It wasn't long before I was confronted by three psychics, one man and two women, after an evening church service. The male psychic started the conversation by saying I had caused quite a stir, and then he asked if I would not say anything against the psychics. I told him that I could not be silent about what they were doing to the people. He responded that he was a Jew. He said he knew that the Bible says to know men by their fruit and he believed that what they were doing was for the good of the people.

I told this man that, being a Jew, he should know about the curses laid upon those who seek mediums and psychics; and furthermore, that the fruit he bore did not come from the same tree as my fruit. He responded with a metaphor, saying that he had a refrigerator which he used every day, although he didn't know how it works.

I said, "You may not know how it works, but if you were a repair man you would know everything about it. If you are going to practice in the spirit realm, you had better know what spirit you are dealing with." They turned and left the church and I never heard from them again.

Just because you may know of things to come does not necessarily mean that you have heard from God. If what you heard truly is from God and you do not give Him the credit, you will be no better than a psychic. The scriptures tell us to test the spirits to know that they are of God.

"Beloved, do not believe every spirit, but test the spirits, whether they are of God; because many false prophets have gone out into the world" (1 John 4:1).

The Power to Prophesy with Angels

The level of the prophet's discernment will be ramped up to a point where the prophets will appear to be talking to themselves. Their appointed angels will be so life-like that at times they will forget that no one else can see or hear them. The manner in which these prophets will speak will be like one translating what the angels are prophesying. The prophets will declare the prophecy in their own language for everyone to hear and understand what is about to take place.

Our enemies will discover that their plans are spoiled every time one of the prophets begin to prophesy. After the prophets expose our enemy's plans accurately each time, plans will be made to shut the mouths of the prophets by beheading them, and more. With news cameras all around the hacked-up bodies of the prophets lying in the streets, the Holy Spirit will miraculously raise them up for the whole world to see. This will cause great fear in the hearts of our enemies so that they will lay down their weapons and surrender unto our God. So be it, Amen!

Revelation 11:3–13 says, "And I will give power to my two witnesses, and they will prophesy one thousand two hundred and sixty days, clothed in sackcloth. These are the two olive trees and the two lamp stands standing before the God of the earth. And if anyone wants to harm them, fire proceeds from their mouth and devours their enemies. And if anyone wants to harm them, he must be killed in this manner. These have power to shut Heaven, so that no rain falls in the days of their prophecy; and they have power over waters to turn them to blood, and to strike the earth with all plagues, as often as they desire.

"When they finish their testimony, the beast that ascends out of the bottomless pit will make war against them, overcome them, and kill them. And their dead bodies will lie in the street of the great city which spiritually is called Sodom and Egypt, where also our Lord was crucified. Then those from the peoples, tribes, tongues, and nations will see their dead bodies three-and-a-half days, and not allow their dead bodies to be put into graves. And those who dwell on the earth will rejoice over them, make merry, and send gifts to one another, because these two prophets tormented those who dwell on the earth.

"Now after the three-and-a-half days, the breath of life from God entered them, and they stood on their feet, and great fear fell on those who saw them. And they heard a loud voice from Heaven saying to them, 'Come up here.' And they ascended to Heaven in a cloud, and their enemies saw them. In the same hour there was a great earthquake, and a tenth of the city fell. In the earthquake seven thousand people were killed, and the rest were afraid and gave glory to the God of Heaven."

God's Prophets and His Angels

"The Revelation of Jesus Christ, which God gave Him to show His servants things which must shortly take place. And He sent and signified it by His angel to His servant John" (Rev. 1:1).

Part of me really wants to share what I have been told regarding the book of Revelation, but I do my best not to teach too much on the topic. There are certain things that I have been shown that I am not at liberty to speak about until such time as His Word has been sent from His throne.

Most everyone thinks that they can figure out an accurate timeline just by comparing the scriptures with the events of today.

There is so much more to know and understand about this wonderful book of prophecy, but there is one thing I will share that I have learned about this great book. I have noticed that the battle cannot begin until the angels of God have delivered His Word and it has been devoured by His prophets.

Once the prophets have His Word in them, the angels will be waiting with great anticipation for the prophets to begin prophesying the words that were sent to them. Until the prophets speak the Word on Earth as it has been declared in Heaven, the angels of God cannot do anything. They lay in wait for the hour, the day, the month, and the year to be released by the word of the prophets.

"So the four angels who had been prepared for the hour and day and month and year were released to kill a third of mankind . . . The angel whom I saw standing . . . swore . . . that there should be delay no longer, but in the days of the sounding of the seventh angel, when he is about to sound, the mystery of God would be finished, as He declared to His servants the prophets" (Rev. 9:15, 10:5–7).

When the angels of the Lord come bringing the word of God in the form that the prophets can digest and understand, only then will they know the will of God and what needs to be spoken on Earth in accordance with His Word in Heaven.

"Then I took the little book out of the angel's hand and ate it, and it was as sweet as honey in my mouth. But when I had eaten it, my stomach became bitter. And he said to me, 'You must prophesy again about many peoples, nations, tongues, and kings'" (Rev. 10:10–11).

After the prophets have the knowledge that they will receive from the angels, a strange thing will begin to happen. The angels will start pleading with the prophets to prophesy the words that were written in the little book that they ate. You see, the angels cannot begin the war until the prophets start prophesying that which God has declared. So what are the things these prophets will be prophesying?

"These have power to shut Heaven, so that no rain falls in the days of their prophecy; and they have power over waters to turn them to blood, and to strike the earth with all plagues, as often as they desire" (Rev. 11:6).

When the enemies of the church realize that these prophets have the ability to bring havoc into their world, they will send out assassins to kill the prophets in order to shut off God's word from being prophesied. After they kill the prophets, they will begin to celebrate the deaths of those who brought the plagues and turned the waters to blood.

"And those who dwell on the earth will rejoice over them, make merry, and send gifts to one another, because these two prophets tormented those who dwell on the earth" (Rev. 11:10).

However, to the startling surprise of the enemies of God, He will raise His prophets from the dead and they will ascend unto Heaven.

"Now after the three-and-a-half days the breath of life from God entered them, and they stood on their feet, and great fear fell on those who saw them. And they heard a loud voice from Heaven saying to them, 'Come up here.' And they ascended to Heaven in a cloud, and their enemies saw them" (Rev. 11:11–12).

I do not think that we truly know the power that we have with our words. Not just in casual conversation, but also when we know that something we have said has a strange feeling attached to it. There have been times when I have experienced His Word come up through me, and as I spoke His Word, to my amazement I felt as though fire were coming out of mouth, even though I was speaking in a mild and calm manner.

Remembering this, I cannot help but tell you about an old prophet that passed on to glory in 1965. His name is William M. Branham and he was God's prophet for that generation. He was used of God as many witnessed the raw power of the Holy Spirit working signs and wonders through his ministry. I have enjoyed studying about his ministry, and there is one event that I think is worth mentioning here.

There was a city where a group of congregations joined together and rented the largest building in town to hold a campaign for Brother Branham, like what we would call a conference today. Before he began ministering, Brother Branham was strongly warned about a man in the town who seemed to always show up and try his best to shut their meetings down.

Brother Branham was not too concerned and just decided to let the Lord deal with the man if he was to have a problem with his preaching on Jesus. Sure enough, as Brother Branham was right in the middle of his sermon, the fellow showed up. He came storming down the aisle headed for the front. The large man was wearing overalls and looked like he could really hurt someone. Brother Branham was a small man on the outside but always had a huge angel at his side.

The man stood at the foot of the stage, shaking his finger and threatening him, claiming Brother Branham was a charlatan. Then he said, "I adjure you, in what name do you do these things?"

Brother Branham very calmly laid down his bible on the pulpit, and he looked straight into the man's eyes and said, "In the name of Jesus Christ, about whom you know very little."

The man dropped dead right where he stood. Brother Branham was not surprised one bit, but everyone else stood in total fear of the Lord. The meetings stretched on for almost a week, and each night the building was filled to the limit.

"Do not touch my anointed ones, and do my prophets no harm" (Ps. 105:15).

I am not suggesting that I am one of the prophets mentioned in the book of Revelation, for I truly believe they will be of a younger generation of men and women. My time has already passed; therefore, I am seeking to train and teach as many young men and women in the prophetic as possible. We have a few now with whom I am very humbled to be associated.

As of January 2016, we have over 506 ministers who have completed PMT's School of Prophetic Knowledge and have received their ordination papers and ministerial licenses. Many of them are working full-time in the ministry and we are needing more ministers every day. All of them are filled with the Holy Spirit and operate in the power and mighty name of Jesus Christ and in the radiant love of our Heavenly Father.

With so many changes taking place in the world today, we all need to know what is happening in the spirit. All of the answers of the universe are within us because if Christ lives within you, you have all of the knowledge.

The challenge is how to get this information from your spirit to your mind. Prophetic knowledge is the key to helping you receive clear interpretation of what God is saying to you. The School of Prophetic Knowledge will help you plan for your ministry and/ or your family's future, plus know what to expect in the coming months and years.

The School of Prophetic Knowledge is a short, 12-DVD course. You can complete this school in two weeks and there is no test or grade to make. Also included is a scripture manual accompanied with your ordination papers and ministerial licenses. We have many positions open for those who are called of God to go into full-time ministry. We are raising up the next generation of God's Generals under the mighty name of Jesus Christ, to lead His people through the spiritual battles that lie ahead of us.

"My brethren, be strong in the Lord and in the power of His might. Put on the whole armor of God that you may be able to stand against the wiles of the devil. For we do not wrestle against flesh and blood, but against principalities, against powers, against the rulers of the darkness of this age, against spiritual hosts of wickedness in the heavenly places. Therefore, take up the whole armor of God, that you may be able to withstand in the evil day, and having done all, to stand" (Eph. 6:10–13).

Chapter 5

My Angelic Encounters

The Prophetic Sign I Will Never Forget

A mysterious and strange spirit came to me when I was only 9 years old, which led me on a lifelong quest for answers. My sister and I had been staying with my grandmother in West, Texas. She had invited my 2-year-old sister and I to come stay with her for 2 weeks during the hot, dry month of June, 1961. Our parents needed to spend some time together just the two of them, so our loving Grandmother Simpson willingly obliged to have us stay with her.

She was so blessed to entertain (or I should say spoil) us with anything and everything we asked for. Having been a widow for many years, she craved to have company, especially her grandchildren. Each day was well planned with all kinds of activities; no grass was going to grow under our feet while we were in her care.

The 2 weeks passed quickly, and the time came for our parents to pick up my sister and me. It was around 7:00 in the evening when the telephone rang. My dad was calling to tell Grandma they were coming to pick us up. This required a 60-mile trip for our parents. While Grandma continued to visit with my dad, a light rain began to fall. Rain in West, Texas is rare; in fact, the average annual rainfall is 19.53 inches (www.usclimatedata.com).

This rain was not only a rare sight, but it brought with it a very strange sensation; it made me feel sad and uncomfortable. All of a sudden a strong impression came upon me and forced me to yield to an urgent message. When I stopped my mind from racing, a voice very clearly said, "There is going to be an accident and it will be fatal."

I immediately began to interrupt my Grandma as she tried to talk to my parents. She kept pushing me away, but I persisted in begging her to let me talk to them. When she hung up the phone I asked her, "Grandmother, why did you not let me talk to them?" She responded, "They will be here in about hour."

With tears in my eyes, I said, "No they won't, they're going to have a wreck." Grandmother did not take me seriously. I'm sure she just thought I didn't want to go home or that I was just tired, but I knew what I heard; the wreck was going to leave me without parents.

I began to pace around the house, pleading with God not to let them die. At one point I became exhausted and I leaned forward, placing my head upon my forearm that was pressed up against the inside of the front door. Suddenly, I remembered reading in the Bible that men of God would envision things they wanted to happen as they prayed, and God would honor their prayers. I started praying and entreating God as I envisioned within my mind my parents just running off the road and no one getting hurt, but I was already too late.

About 20 minutes later, my dad's four brothers came walking into the house. Their faces looked very strained and none of them would look directly at me. One of my uncles sat down by the telephone and just stared at it. Eventually, he called the hospital. He was trying to find out where my parents were located, or at least that is what I thought was happening. Supposedly, he was speaking with the hospital receptionist, repeating everything she was saying so everyone could hear.

Then he tearfully said, "So the wife was killed but the husband lived and is in shock?" My dad's youngest brother was standing behind me throughout the phone call with his hands placed firmly on my shoulders. As soon as my uncle repeated the condition of my parents I broke down crying. My 2-year-old sister turned and began trying to console me. I kept telling her, as tears were streaming down my face, "You don't understand. You're too young to know what is going on."

Looking Back at What I Have Learned

I realized much later that my uncle pretended to be calling the hospital because none of my uncles could bear telling me to my face what had happened. There good way to break bad news.

A couple of years passed and I finally got up the nerve to ask my grandmother if she remembered me pleading with her while she was on the phone with my parents. Did she recall I told her they would have a wreck? She washed dishes while looking out the window when she answered me. Without turning toward me, she said, "Yes, I remember."

Then she asked me, "How did you know they would have a wreck?" As I walked away, I told her I didn't know. The way she said it made me feel as if something was wrong with me, like I was not normal.

One of my mother's brothers helped me understand from which side of my family the prophetic gift had been passed down from generation to generation. While my sister and I were with our grandmother, my mother's oldest brother was on a summer vacation with his family in Colorado. Years later, while telling me his story, he indicated he too had a revelation about my mother's death. He said he suddenly experienced a great urge to pack up everything and head back home to Texas. He knew in his spirit that something was wrong with his baby sister. They still had a few days of fun scheduled, but he knew they had to go. So early the next morning, they packed up their gear and started the long trip home.

When they came upon the Texas border, the highway patrol slowed everyone down and pulled over a few cars. When my uncle approached the roadblock, they motioned for him to pull over and a patrolman asked my uncle for his driver's license. Once the officer knew who my uncle was, he told him about the accident that had taken my mother's life. Another patrolman was ordered to escort them the rest of the way home.

This, too, I find interesting: as far back as I can remember, my mother would tell me that I would die when I turned twenty-seven years old. It didn't bother me when she did. I was too young to give it much thought, but I did not forget it. I guess she had a vision that she would lose me at twenty-seven. Her interpretation turned out to be partly correct; she was twenty-seven at the time of the wreck. Her words haunted me for many years after she died, until my twenty-eighth birthday had passed. I didn't think about it too much after that birthday, but I learned a lot from this sad experience.

From that point on, I searched to find out how I knew in advance that my mother and father were going to be involved in a fatal accident. Why did the rain bring such an awful feeling, like it was speaking a disturbing truth to me? Where was the voice coming from, and who was it? Was it God or Satan? Could it have been an angel, or maybe a demon? Why did the impression come so strongly, to the point I felt there was no way I could stop it?

Throughout my teenage years I would learn about all kinds of spiritual methods and teachings on how a person can know of things to come, but nothing sounded quite right.

It wasn't until years later, when I was baptized in the Holy Spirit, that the great Teacher revealed to me how we sometimes know of things to come.

"However, when He, the Spirit of truth, has come, He will guide you into all truth; for He will not speak on His own authority, but whatever He hears He will speak; and He will tell you things to come" (John 16:13).

The Most Important Thing I Learned

It is not enough to hear the voice of God; you must know what He means. Furthermore, it takes many years to develop the knowledge and understanding of the spiritual gifts of the Holy Spirit. For this reason, I encourage those who believe they may have a spiritual gift to find someone with the same gifting and calling and not leave their side. You cannot receive the double portion of the anointing as Elisha did if you ignore the knowledge of God's appointed Elijah for you.

"Now Elijah took his mantle, rolled it up, and struck the water; and it was divided this way and that, so that the two of them crossed over on dry ground. And so it was, when they had crossed over, that Elijah said to Elisha, 'Ask! What may I do for you, before I am taken away from you?'

"Elisha said, 'Please let a double portion of your spirit be upon me.' So he said, 'You have asked a hard thing. Nevertheless, if you see me when I am taken from you, it shall be so for you; but if not, it shall not be so'" (2 Kings 2:8–10).

The Story of a Mail Order Prophet

As I recall, in the early part of November 1989, I walked into my home to make a quick lunch before returning back to work. As I ate my lunch, I turned on the television, and to my surprise, I saw a commercial advertising a 900 number to call in for a reading from a psychic. Focusing in on every word, I watched intently, wondering what in the world it was.

Right after the commercial ended, God spoke. To my amazement, He said, "I want you to do that!" Stunned, I questioned our Lord, first checking to make sure it was His Spirit according to 1 John 4:1–5. I knew that God was against anyone operating under the spirits that psychics use to do what they do (Ref. Deuteronomy 18:9–14).

What did He want me to do, go on television, get a 900 number, or just offer myself as a vessel for Him to speak through? I was already giving face-to-face prophecies. To give someone a word from our Lord and not be able to see them or touch them seemed impossible.

For the next few days I wrestled with this experience. There were so many variables of what He could be asking me to do, I questioned, "Do I really want to do this?" As I was praying a few days later, the Holy Spirit reminded me of Jacob, who wrestled until his hip was taken out of socket. Not wanting to put myself into a similar position, I surrendered to the call and tested it.

Starting with the only form of exposure I could financially afford, I made myself available to the people for a prophetic word through a small ad in the *The Christian Informer*, a local Christian newspaper. The ad read: "Personal Prophecy, words of knowledge and wisdom for you in this lifetime, call ___ ____." The first issue in which the ad ran was November 1990.

Approximately 3 days later, I received my first phone call. I was so nervous; I did not know what I was going to do. The man said he wanted a word for his wife and himself. Not feeling the presence of God anywhere, I froze; however, to put their request off, I quickly asked the man if I could send him and his wife their word from God on an audio cassette tape. He gave me his address and I hung up the phone.

Feeling some relief, I exhaled, and then the reality of the commitment I had just made hit me. I told the man I would record their word from God on a cassette tape and mail it to them. How was I going to do this? Fear just climbed all over me, so I quickly began to pray. All of sudden, the Holy Spirit firmly said to me, "You either hear me or you don't!"

I knew this was a breaking point for me. I had to either believe or disbelieve that I could hear His voice. The decision I made is obvious; had I chosen to be a disbeliever you would not be reading this book. The next day I began to seek God for a word for this couple, and I was praying harder than ever. The whole time I was wrestling with the thought that I had to get this right or I could mess these people's lives up.

The pressure was extremely intense. What if I was wrong? What would they do to me? Finally, I had the words recorded; I only needed to mail the tape. As I stood in front of the mail slot at the post office, my fingers did not want to let go of the package holding the recording of God's word. Eventually, I let go and thought to myself, "Well, this is either God or someone needs to stick a fork in me, because I am done." That day, I officially became a Mail Order Prophet, and my, how things have changed over the past decades!

Getting back to my business, I forgot all about the ad until I was home for lunch one day and noticed the light flashing on my telephone recorder. As I strained to listen to the hysterical man on the recording, it was very difficult to understand what he was saying. I did, however, manage to clearly hear him say that he had received the word and his pastor would be calling me soon. Once again fear struck me, and all I could think about was how badly I was going to be chewed out and what might happen if he called my pastor.

Preparing for a Pastor's Rebuke

Each time I was at home, I found myself dodging the telephone messages on my telephone recorder in fear of what I might hear.

All kinds of horrible things went through my mind as to what may come of the dreaded conversation.

One day, I rushed into the house to pick up something and I heard the phone ring. Without thinking, I picked up the telephone and on the other end I heard, "This is Pastor Gill Hawks from Rockwall, Texas."

Squeezing the phone with one hand, the nails on my other hand were digging into the counter top as I waited for a harsh tongue-lashing. He mentioned that one of his parishioners had requested a word and that he had listened to it. As my anxiety peaked, to my surprise he said, "I would like you to send me four prophecies: one for me, my wife, and two sons."

Within a couple of days, I found time to record what I heard from our Lord, and I mailed the prophecy tapes right away. I had not told anyone about the newspaper ad or that I had received requests; I really did not think they would understand. I even prayed, asking God if He would allow me to stop running the ad before someone found out.

It was a Wednesday night after I had mailed out those four tapes, and it was my turn to bring the message at our local church. As I sat in the church pew studying my bible, my Senior Pastor, Ray Thompson, came to me and said, "There is a Pastor Gill Hawks from Rockwall, Texas here and he wants to talk with you."

Fear washed over me as perspiration began to cover my fore-head. Not knowing what Pastor Hawks was going to say, my mind filled in the blanks with the vision of him attacking me with gnashing teeth and lashing tongue; I needed a solution and fast. Then it came to me: pastors love to preach and teach, so I decided to defuse his anger by asking him to take the pulpit in my place.

My pastor agreed with a questioning look on his face, but I did not give up any information about why I was making this unusual request. Pastor Hawks was truly blessed that I asked him to take the pulpit; I felt all was okay now.

After everyone was seated, I introduced Pastor Gill Hawks and handed over the microphone. Before I could sit down he started off with the ad he had seen in the Christian Monitor, a newspaper for the Dallas, Fort Worth Metroplex area. Then Pastor Hawks began to talk about calling me and requesting four prophecy tapes for his family.

As I began to melt in the pew, sliding slowly downward in the hope of making myself invisible, my pastor turned around in his pew just a few rows ahead of me and glared holes through me. It seemed as though the entire congregation turned to look at me with expressions that communicated a vast array of thoughts, from confusion to anger and everything in between.

After Pastor Hawks gave his report about his prophecy being wonderfully accurate, I began to straighten up and I felt myself sitting tall in the pew. Pastor Hawk's wife was with him, and he gave a raving report about her word as she gave a continual nod of approval throughout his report. By the time he had finished his account of the prophecies his family had received, the people and pastor of my church were actually smiling at me. It was great, and I was blessed by how everything had worked out.

My Guardian Angel and the Lady Bug

I have been blessed to have experienced a number of angelic encounters along this wonderful journey with our Lord and Savior, and I have a couple of stories to share. I have been in some tight spots in my life, but each time God's favor has kept me from being seriously injured. There have been times when, financially, we were in so much trouble that we were about to lose everything, but the Holy Spirit sent an angel to show me the way to fix the situation.

Many of you know that I have had a real craving for motorcycles for most of my life. I believe we can all agree that riding motorcycles is a risky endeavor. A number of times my friends and

I got together to go riding; however, we referred to this activity as dodging cars, which is a large part of the sport. Riding a motorcycle on a crowded interstate is like running with the bulls.

If I had to choose my most favored motorcycle from all the ones I have owned, it would be the "Lady Bug." Back in the day I was frequently adding special parts, customizing my ride to my liking. I recall in the summer of 2001, I had received a package from UPS and I knew it had to be my new highway pegs. These pegs are made for stretching out and resting your legs while riding down the highway.

After I had installed them, I thought I needed to go and try them out. I had a number of different routes I had created over the years, and this one needed to be a long ride with lots of curves. Choosing the Lake Worth route, I headed out to make sure that when I took the curves my pegs would not drag the pavement.

As I exited off the interstate, making my way around the lake, I noticed that my left peg was grinding the pavement on each turn. At one sharp curve, I decided to look down and see how bad it was. Now, anyone who rides motorcycles knows the rule; wherever you look is where your motorcycle will go. As I came into one long sweeping curve, I took a chance and leaned over to check out my left peg. Big mistake!

When I finally realized I had messed up, it was too late; very quickly, I over-corrected my error and I landed in the ditch. When it was all over I found myself with a 750-pound mountain of hot metal on top of me. Fortunately, the ground was sandy and soft from a recent rain, which kept the bike from crushing me; however, I was not able to get out from under its weight.

Lying there with my leg getting very warm from the exhaust pipes, I began to accept the fact that I needed help. This lake road was not well traveled, but fortunately, in just a few minutes I heard a car coming around the corner. Slowing down, the driver very quickly rolled the window down and this nice lady asked if she needed to go for help.

Embarrassed and still not ready to let go of my pride, I thanked her but declined her assistance. I kept trying to dig my way out, but it was just not enough to get free. Then another lady stopped and said she had a mobile phone and she could call for help; once again I declined.

Finally, I gave in and prayed these exact words: "Lord, I need a hand. Please help me get out of here." In just a few seconds, a jeep came around the bend and a small fellow stuck his head out and asked if I needed help. Without hesitation I said, YES! As he walked toward me, I noticed he only had one arm and I began to laugh out loud. He started chuckling wanting to know what was so funny.

I told him I had just said a prayer asking the Lord to send me a hand and then you came around the corner. We both laughed for just a second and then everything got really eerie and foggy; time seemed to speed up, and in a split second I was standing outside of the ditch and holding up my motorcycle.

After gaining my bearings, I turned to thank the fellow for helping me, but he was already gone. I do not remember him pulling on the bike or me getting up off the ground. I believe you will agree with me that sending me a one-armed angel after I had prayed to our Father to send me a hand reveals the measure of His divine humor.

The Angel Spoke to Me

A few years prior to the "Lady Bug" experience, I was visited by a very tall angel who spoke to me and told me what he was sent to do for me.

I will start from the beginning: I was in my study, busy straightening up and picking up books and magazines that I had been going through for the past week. All of sudden a form started taking shape in my doorway. It is rather difficult to explain how it took shape, but if you remember the old popular TV series "Star Trek," it might help you understand how the angel appeared. Remember what it looked like when the members of the ship were being transported and they would say, "Beam me up Scotty"? Well, that was exactly what it looked like, and it did not take very long for all the digital pieces to fill into the empty space that quickly became the form of the angel.

He was so tall I could not see his face because it was hidden behind the top part of the door casing. He did move but not very much; he just straightened up a little after he completed his transformation. I was scared and didn't know if this was an angel from

God or a demon taking on the appearance of an angel. Then he spoke with an audible voice saying, "I will tell you what you need to know and I will prosper you." Well, that settled it; he had to be a demon.

You see, back then my doctrine was much different than it is now and we did not believe that ministers were to have anything, especially money. The poorer you were, the more spiritual you became. Anytime we had more than we needed for a day or so we gave it away lest it found a way into our hearts. Without even thinking, I raised my voice, stuck out my pointer finger and rebuked the demon/angel. He vanished faster than he had appeared.

Immediately, I began pulling all my ministry books and bible out and I began preparing a message entitled, "The Spirit of Divination." The message started with this verse: "Now it happened, as we went to prayer, that a certain slave girl possessed with a spirit of divination met us, who brought her masters much profit by fortune-telling" (Acts 16:16).

You see, I knew this scripture well because I had been leading a campaign against the #900 psychics, and I just knew this had to be the same spirit that wanted to get into me. I was determined to keep him out and chase him far away from me.

At that time, we had a Saturday morning radio program, and I preached against that foul spirit live over the radio. Then that night I was scheduled to preach at a conference in the Dallas Convention Hall by the Dallas/Fort Worth International Airport, preaching the second part of the series. The next morning, I preached the third and final sermon completing the three-part series. After we had the series complete and nicely packaged, we began to offer the series in our newsletter.

A few weeks had gone by and we seemingly supernaturally started losing most of our supporters, and money to pay our bills stopped coming in. This all happened in 1993, just before the Thanksgiving holidays. We were flat broke and had no food. Attendance in our little church was dwindling, and I was forced to go to the local food bank just so we could have a few groceries. My wife had just given birth to Savannah and we were getting very frightened that we may soon be without a place to live.

Of course, I had been praying my heart out to God for answers, but the heavens seemed to be closed to my prayers. After one of our evening services as I was walking across the parking lot, God spoke. He said, "If you are going to preach about demons then let the demons support you; I called you to preach about hearing me and my messages." Well that is all I needed to know, or so I thought.

The next morning, I told God I would destroy the master tapes to this message about the spirit of divination, and I would call everyone and request them to burn their copies. Then I began to plead with Him to help me. After a day or two He spoke these words: "I sent you the one to help you and you ran him off." I knew I had messed up big time.

That night I lay awake in our bed, musing before the Holy Spirit, looking for a way I could get this angel back. Suddenly I had a revelation that gave me an idea. You know how when you walk by a place where there is known evil activity going on and you can feel the presence of demons? Well, my theory was that angels must hang around places where God and His people gather.

It was four o'clock in the morning, and I jumped out of the bed waking my wife, telling her I was going to the Tabernacle. She wanted to know why but fell back to sleep while I was excitedly telling her about my plan.

Back then our motto was "Pray, Preach, and Prophesy"; which came from a teaching the Holy Spirit taught me on how to usher in the spirit of prophecy. The revelation then was that if you prayed to find out what to preach, and you preached what you were told during prayer, the angel of prophecy would show up to minister for you. Now I knew what to preach, so I would deliver the message until my prophetic angel came down with my word. Then I would prophesy to the angels gathered in the Tabernacle and they would have to do His Word according to this Scripture: "Bless the Lord, you His angels, who excel in strength, who do His word, heeding the voice of His word" (Ps. 103:20).

Preaching and Prophesying to Angels

I had finally found God and His revelation, and the answer to why everything in my life was falling apart. He had sent me an angel, which I mistook to be a demon, and I ran him off. God had sent the angel to help me financially, who spoke to me these words: "I will tell you what you need to know and I will prosper you."

God had graciously allowed me the insight of what I needed to do in order to receive the promise within this verse of Scripture: "But to which of the angels has He ever said: 'Sit at My right hand, till I make your enemies your footstool?' Are they not all ministering spirits sent forth to minister FOR those who will inherit salvation?" (Heb. 1:13–14).

When I got to the Tabernacle early that morning, I rummaged around in the office looking for a blank tape to put in the recorder. I wanted to have a copy of my prophecy. I had been doing a lot of studying on angels after that experience where the angel appeared in my doorway. I figured if they are sent to us from God, we best know something about them.

As I made my way to the pulpit where the tape recording system was, I put the blank tape in the recorder. My theory was that God's angels could always be found wherever God's people gathered. I knew from scripture that whatever the Lord spoke in Heaven had to manifest on Earth as it is written: "Your kingdom come, your will be done on Earth as it is in Heaven" (Matt. 6:10).

All I had to do was speak whatever he was saying from heaven and his angels would have to go do his word. The angelic hosts of God have been commanded to do his will on Earth, as it has been proclaimed in Heaven. This is a huge breakthrough for the body of Christ! If you can find God and his word, and you speak his word on earth as it has been spoken from his throne, his angels will go do his Word.

It does not matter whose voice it is that declares his rhema word; for His angels know His will for you and when the word is spoken his angels excel to do his will. All that matters now is that His word is proclaimed; then everything will change because his angels will do His word.

With that in mind and the tape in the recorder, with the sound system live throughout the sanctuary, I began to preach the message from my heart. Not seeing one angel sitting in the pews, I continued to preach as if the room was packed out. Finally, His word came, delivered by the angel that had been appointed unto me a few years prior. This angel is God's messenger appointed to minister for me, ascending and descending from His throne, delivering His prophetic word for whomever is in need of a word from God. This night the word was for ME!

I can just imagine what my angel thought when he landed in the Tabernacle sanctuary and saw all these other angels filling up the room. I could hear in my spirit him say "What are you all doing here?" And they all replied, "Waiting on the word of the Lord so we know what to do." When these types of spiritual things happen to you, it is difficult to explain in detail how something like this transpires.

Now I was ready for the final results and blessings from all my praying, hearing, and obeying. Satisfied that I had my word of prophecy, I shut everything off and went home, leaving the Tabernacle knowing in my spirit it was finished. I had done all that I could do; it was time to sit back and patiently wait upon His angel to do the work.

Two weeks went by and we still had faith that His word was going to work for us. Then the day finally came when someone was at my door. As I opened it, there stood a middle aged man in a suit and tie. He introduced himself, and all I remember is that his first name was Harold.

I invited him into are humble little home, and he sat down. Without hesitation, he began to state his reason for coming to visit us without introduction. He asked if I knew of a list of men who I had played high school football with and said he represented them. We talked about each one and we had fond memories of the "good ole days." Then he got to the point of his coming as he reached into his coat pocket and pulled out a check for $50,000. I was floored and utterly shocked, needless to say.

It was evident the angel God had originally sent me (that I had foolishly ran off) was now back. The evidence can only be found in the favor of God's unrelenting love and grace. From that time forward, this ministering spirit has been there for this ministry many times over.

Angels for Today: Encountering Angels

Angels are being appointed today; they are being sent forth to minister for you according to Hebrews 1:14.

During the month of December, 2012, I began to notice that as I prophesied each day, God would begin to instruct me to make bold proclamations about almost every person I prophesied over. In the beginning of the month it was just a few, but by the middle of the month it began to increase. Now it seems He is appointing His angels to everyone who desires to hear His word.

It was about this same time that I realized something big was about to begin. God is imparting so many spiritual gifts, while at the same time commissioning an angel to minister for the one who receives a prophecy. People, a wave of declarations are being made in the heavens, preparing the Body of Christ for a huge move of the Holy Spirit. It is not going to matter how the economy is or what legislation is being made in our governments. What is happening in the heavens will make the headlines. We will read something about the signs and wonders flowing throughout the world on a daily basis.

One day recently, as I was walking to my office, a strong vision came upon me. Suddenly, several secret service agents were interrogating me. They desperately wanted to know how all these Christians were able to know where to go to meet up with their like kind. Massive numbers of Christians were being assembled in unlikely places, drawn by the power of the Holy Spirit without e-mail, phone calls, or public announcements. Only by the supernatural leading of the Holy Spirit, people were being brought together at various specified locations.

Again, the agents began to push for answers, wanting to know how we were getting the message out to everyone. They indicated they were monitoring the internet and tracking cellular devices when they noticed thousands of dots congregating in various locations. On their screen, these dots represented the governments' unique electronic tracking methods planted in the people's phones and other tracking devices; that is when they became alarmed that a mob was forming.

Special authorities were immediately dispatched to investigate what was going on. When they reported back that there were large numbers of people gathering, holding some kind of religious services, the agents became greatly concerned not knowing how the Christian people were notified of these meetings without the government knowing. They also reported that a very strange magnetic power was detected over the entire area, and people were claiming to be healed and seeing angels as if they all were on drugs or drunk. The authorities reported that people were falling down, while others were screaming and dancing like wild fiends.

The agents were polite as they continued questioning me. I could tell they were very scared and concerned because of their inability to understand how we all were receiving the same message to meet at the same places in the same hour, without them knowing in advance. It seemed to the agents that everything was very orderly and was being conducted by someone whom they could not trace.

Frustrated with my answers, they continued to ask if I would tell them who the leader of this organization was and how the leader was able to communicate to everyone without being detected. Each time I would reply, "We know by the Holy Spirit, who leads us to wherever the Spirit of Jesus is healing us and empowering us with His word." They even offered me a large sum of money to tell them the truth, for they did not believe me that it was the Holy Spirit calling us together Spirit to spirit. The exact word they used was "rubbish" regarding my answers on how we were called together.

After many hours, they asked me if I would teach them how all of this worked. They said that if they did not get an answer soon about how these events were being simulated, they were going to lose their jobs and the entire branch of the government could be dismantled and turned over to another segment of the government.

As the vision closed and I came back to my natural self, God dropped into me His word: Begin teaching, preaching, and imparting His angels and spiritual gifts accordingly. This revelation is huge and life-changing, and will empower the Body of Christ to launch out into the power of John 14:12. "Most assuredly, I say to you, he who believes in me, the works that I do he will do also; and greater works than these he will do, because I go to My Father."

Chapter 6

The Missing Link to Saving Our Children

Putting Our Children on the Right Path

"And so we have the prophetic word confirmed, which you do well to heed as a light that shines in a dark place, until the day dawns and the morning star rises in your hearts" (2 Pet. 1:19).

Jesus is our example, and we do our best as His Church to follow all the requirements set before us. From witnessing to disciplining, those who are called to be a part of His Body are trained to follow His path. Recognizing that even Jesus was baptized in water, we too practice water baptism. However, there is one very important act of Christianity we do not practice in accordance with our Lord and Savior.

We honor Jesus with our traditional celebrations of His birth and His resurrection; however, we seem to be blinded to one major step in finding our purpose in life. We are celebrated at our birth and somewhere further in our life we may be dedicated to the Lord.

Some practice dedication of their children to the Lord while they are still young, while others have their priest baptize their children when they are still in their infancy. All these practices have some form of traditional value, but we are still missing the most important part of putting our children on the right path.

Our Children's Calling and Purpose

Many of us wonder why our children have to go through a time of rebellion. Sometimes a strong demonic oppression takes them down a path of hellish experiences that can tear a family apart. When parents lose their children to the evil one even though they raised them in the ways of God, they feel the teachings of the Church have failed them. Frustrated and sad, parents will quote Proverbs as their evidence of them raising their children up according to God's plan: "Train up a child in the way he should go, and when he is old he will not depart from it" (Prov. 22:6).

Losing our children to the evil one does not need, nor have to happen. If we add the missing link in our teaching them how to walk in the footsteps of our Christ Jesus, I know His word will keep our children safe and in His perfect will. With that said, we also know that our children will be tested by Satan and his demons just as Christ was tempted by the evil one (see Luke 4:1–13).

The difference is Jesus knew His calling and purpose in this life. Not only did Jesus know His purpose, so did His mother and many others. His path had already been preordained, and our lives should be just the same. There should be no reason for the devil to have his way with our children. We should grow up knowing in advance what our calling and purpose in life will be.

Sowers of His Word

Over the many years that I have been involved in the prophetic ministry, I have learned many things, but I have not had a large platform to share what has been revealed to me. I realize that I am nothing more than an old plow shear, called to break the hard ground, preparing it for others to water. One day the sowers of His word will plant this practice in the souls of Christians everywhere through their gifted teachings, as others will come behind them to reap the harvest of this labor.

Now is the time to turn the revelation of the plow over to the sowers of His word. Then we can begin equipping this next generation with the power of His word, going before them as a lamp unto their feet, keeping them out of the pitfalls of the enemy. What is the revelation, the missing link, the one thing that will guide our children into their calling and purpose?

It is simple, really. It is the Word of God—the most important thing in a Christian's life. Why then do we keep that word from being spoken over our children? I am talking about their personal prophecy. Their gift and calling of God begins with a word of prophecy being proclaimed over them, even as early as eight days of age.

Why not prophesy over them while they are still in their mother's womb? Why is it that we wait until our children have already been spoken over by Satan and his influences thousands of times before we allow the personal words of our Heavenly Father to be pronounced over them? It is not enough to just say, "I give my son or daughter over to the Lord." We need to know what they will be, what they will do, and what their purpose in life is all about.

Do you recall when Jesus was only eight days old and His mother and father took Him to the temple? There was a man there, named Simeon, that said he had waited his entire life knowing that he would not be able to go on until he had prophesied over the Messiah. He blessed God and said that Jesus would be "A light to bring revelation to the Gentiles, and the glory of [Your] people Israel."

There was also a woman there named Anna who prophesied to all she met who were looking for redemption that Jesus was the one. (See Luke 2:22–38.)

Following this same pattern will sow into our God-given covering of protection, which allows us to do what we have been created to do.

Prophecy Over Children

Even if you missed the opportunity for your children to be prophesied over at eight days of age, it's never too late. This is our missing link, people! This is the part of the pattern to have our children washed in the watering of His word. No longer should we allow our children to flounder around in this world, wandering around in darkness, waiting for the light to come and illuminate their path so they can see where they are to go and what they are to do.

Early on in this ministry, God had me begin asking parents if I could speak a word over their children. Many pastors have been more than gracious, allowing me to prophesy over the children. It has always made a special service for everyone, especially the parents who fight to hold back their tears as they see their little one having His word of prophecy spoken and recorded.

It has been one of my most rewarding experiences in life to have young men and women come to my home and share with me the prophecy I imparted to them, even when they were so young at the time that they didn't know who I was or what I was telling them. It is such a special part of my life and ministry to see what God has accomplished through this one act of obedience. To be used as a vessel for God, to speak life's destiny into a baby or young person's life, is so rewarding. I just pray I live long enough to hear more of these testimonies.

When I Get to Heaven

People say that when we get to Heaven we can ask Jesus for the answers to spiritual questions that we may have. I ask, why would we need to wait until then? Wouldn't it be more helpful for us if we had the answers to these questions now? What good will it do for us to know when we are in Heaven? We need answers to questions now!

I have found that we can pray and ask Jesus now and receive His answers for today. Scripture says, "My sheep know My voice" (John 10:27). That means we ought to know the answers because Scripture also tells us, "You have an anointing from the Holy One, and you know all things" (1 John 2:20).

"'For there is nothing hidden which will not be revealed, nor has anything been kept secret but that it should come to light. If anyone has ears to hear, let him hear.' Then He said to them, 'Take heed what you hear. With the same measure you use, it will be measured to you; and to you who hear, more will be given'" (Mark 4:22–24).

We can have the answers to spiritual questions, but many believers have difficulty with this if their doctrine does not teach this truth. It is not wise to limit God in the ways He speaks to us. In the Holy Scriptures, He tells us that the Holy Spirit will teach us and that we can hear His voice and know His ways. Once we learn to hear and trust His voice, no one will ever talk us out of our experiences with Him.

"These things we also speak, not in words which man's wisdom teaches but which the Holy Spirit teaches, comparing spiritual things with spiritual. But the natural man does not receive the things of the Spirit of God, for they are foolishness to him; nor can he know them, because they are spiritually discerned" (1 Cor. 2:13–14).

One Head, One Body

I cry out for the churches today because we are lacking important elements of our faith. Over the years, vital members of the Body of Christ have been amputated by carnal men who have removed the apostles, prophets, spiritual gifts, and large portions of the Holy Scriptures. Many parts of the body have been removed, leaving only the navel. We are back to the beginning of nothing. However, over the past few decades God has been grooming and reattaching these missing parts back into the Body of Christ. When our body is fully mended we will become unstoppable, and when God moves, we, His people, will move as one complete unit.

Whenever God speaks, the Holy Spirit will move through His body to make the word happen for His people today. It is important to remember that there is only one head of the Church. Each and every group of God's people should have someone leading them who is totally obedient to God's voice. He or she should also have the wisdom to know God's ways. Anyone who leads God's people must have an ear to hear what the Holy Spirit is saying to them.

This is the only true way for the congregations to follow Christ as a body of believers. If the congregation of believers follows the will and direction of man rather than Jesus, they are making man the head and not Jesus. Christ is the only true head of the Church, while the Holy Spirit acts like the nervous system. Whenever God speaks from Heaven, the Holy Spirit goes searching for someone who will set aside their desires and follow the sound of His voice. We cannot bring the Body of Christ through what is ahead of us if we are not allowing the Holy Spirit to lead us.

When the Power of God Fills the Church

When we get out of the way of the Holy Spirit and allow Him to rule over the Church again, signs and wonders will be in the midst of our gatherings. People will not believe except they see signs and wonders. Jesus said, "The works that I do, you shall do greater" (John 14:12).

Jesus is still a miracle worker. How is it possible to do greater works than Jesus? Because he now lives within all of us and is sharing his power with those whom He can trust. He will send the Holy Spirit to make contact with our spirit, calling and commissioning us to do the things that He needs done on Earth. If we are willing to obey His voice and trust in His ways, all of our troubles will no longer be ours. By His grace, our troubles will begin to melt away. "If you abide in me, and my words abide in you, you will ask what you desire, and it shall be done for you" (John 15:7).

If you have Christ, who is all-knowing, who has conquered Heaven and Hell and now lives within you, then you have all the answers to all of your troubles. There is no problem too big for God, but we must be willing to seek Him until we find His prophetic word for our lives and for the lives of those who trust us. When you obey exactly what He has told you to do then you will know all will be okay.

However, too many Christians are going the way of the Pharisees, the very kind of religious folk Jesus condemned. He called them snakes, vipers, and hypocrites. It is so easy to fall into the same trap they were led into. The Spirit groans within us, for it knows the right way to go. The problem most people have with following Jesus all the way is that they are afraid that if they start hearing His voice, He will ask them to do something they are not willing to do. They fear they will not be received by their religious leaders and will lose all their friends.

"You search the Scriptures, for in them you think you have eternal life; and these are they which testify of me. But you are not willing to come to me that you may have life" (John 5:39–40).

What kind of life is Jesus talking about? The abundant life. You search the scriptures because you think you will find eternal life within them, but remember, the Pharisees knew the scriptures. In fact, in order to become a Pharisee, you had to commit the first five books of what is now our bible to memory. They even wore a box filled with the scriptures on their forehead as an outward symbol. The size of their box indicated how much scripture they had memorized, yet even with all their knowledge they did not know the Messiah when He came to them.

Have you ever known anyone who could quote scripture after scripture after scripture, but they were blind as a bat when it came to seeking the will of God? Jesus is saying that you cannot find Him just by memorizing scriptures. The scriptures testify about Him and His works so that you will know Him when He speaks to you and shows you what you must do. Scripture is a "tuning fork." It reveals the personality and character of Christ. You need to feed upon the Holy Bible, for it is the "bread of life." You need to stay in the scriptures to keep your ears in tune with His voice as He guides you into the life He has for you.

It took a long time for the Church to believe that scripture from Genesis to Revelation is the inherent word of God and everything that is recorded happened as recorded. Christ is taking us to another level of faith so that we will "hear" Him. Anyone can read about Jesus, but to know Him personally requires knowing His voice.

There is a lot more to the church than just having the knowledge of the scriptures. We have become a people who have been educated in a system of education to read the Holy Spirit as if it were any other textbook. Many teach that if you can memorize the Holy Bible then you will become all-knowing and all-powerful. That is not so. The Pharisees and Sadducees thought the same thing and look where it got them. In order to receive the power of

Christ, you must be willing to seek God, hear His words, and do whatever He asks you to do no matter the cost.

What God does for you will be different than what He does for someone else. What He speaks to you will be different than what He speaks to another. The way He uses you will be different than the way He uses others. He gives us all what we need according to His will for us individually; he did not create us to be clones. Each one of us has a unique and special gift and our spirits are different from one another. However, we have the same Father. We need to be able to identify what we have been created to do and then do it.

I was born again as a child, and by the grace of God, He showed me what I needed. He gave me direction of what I should do. I was ignorant regarding the scriptures when God called me into the ministry. I respected the bible, but I was ignorant of its value. I knew I needed to learn what it was all about, so I began to study everything I could about God and living in His will.

I began to recognize that many times I had similar encounters as those recorded in the bible. I read in the scriptures about hearing the voice of Jesus and it was like revelation smacked me in the face. Now I knew where that small, still voice was coming from and who it was that was speaking to me in the times I needed help. I was doing things in my life by the Spirit before I read that it was the Holy Spirit whom was given to us according to the Holy Scriptures. I was hearing His voice before I knew that Jesus said, "My sheep know my voice." It is not in your intelligence. It is not how much you know but *who* you know and *who* you are willing to follow that makes your life whole.

People today are looking for a man to follow. Many people will ask, "Who is your mentor? Who is your spiritual father?" My mentor is the Holy Spirit. My father is Father God. Still they ask, "Who is your teacher?" Scripture makes it very clear: "Do not call anyone on Earth your father; for one is your Father, He who is in Heaven. And do not be called teachers; for one is your Teacher, the Christ" (Matt. 23:9–10).

Dying to Yourself

Many people need answers to their situations and their problems, and they are concerned about their children and their future. They pray continually to God, not realizing that it is time for them to let God handle their cares. We should be a people who are unmoved by what happens in the world, yet we find ourselves being sucked into all the worries and troubles of this life. When bad things happen, we search for reasons why. Perhaps we were in the wrong place at the wrong time. Maybe we are just allowing all of the things in this life to create tension and pressure within us.

It is important to remember that whatever you are facing, it is not your problem if you will give it to God! What God will do in your life once you let go of it, will absolutely amaze you. God will begin to move certain people into your path and guide you into a place where you will reap the harvest without doing anything but praying, hearing, and obeying!

This peaceful release is what God really wants from us. The biggest problem with mankind is that we want to be in control. We want to control our lives, circumstances, other people, and most of all God. It is our sinful nature that drives us to be this way. We must let go and let God. When we do, we find that all things work out just as God has willed.

This life is only a "blink of an eye" in comparison to eternity. We have a difficult time understanding the concept of eternity, where there is no beginning and no end. When you consider Heaven and eternity, all of the problems of this life seem to fade away. They become far less important when looking at them from this perspective. We should not take this world so seriously, because this life is not really what we are living for.

Chapter 7

His Anointed Fragrance of Knowledge

"Now thanks be to God who always leads us in triumph in Christ, and through us diffuses the fragrance of His knowledge in every place. For we are to God the fragrance of Christ among those who are being saved and among those who are perishing" (2 Cor. 2:14–15).

With the fragrance of Christ's Spirit, you can accomplish many things. There are varieties of fragrances being released from our Lord's throne, which carry a vast assortment of signs and wonders. With each fragrance, He diffuses a new and different anointing specially scented to accomplish His will. With each anointing a specific angel cleaves to the person upon whom the fragrance is placed. The angel stands in waiting next to the person who has been drawn to them by the fragrance. As soon as the person steps into the fragrance, the anointing is consummated, creating for a short time a new anointing purposed to do amazing signs and wonders in the time given. Jesus said, "Unless you people see signs and wonders, you will by no means believe" (John 4:48).

There are limitations in the timeframe allotted for this anointing to be used for God's glory. You need to be aware of this one major issue. If you do not minister quickly while under the anointing, the angel will leave you as quickly as the fragrance dissipates and sometimes that is measured in seconds. Haven't you been in a situation where you knew within yourself that if you followed the inner tugging of your heart then something wonderful would happen?

The anointing is much different than the gifts of the Holy Spirit, for when a spiritual gift is given unto you it cannot be taken back (see Romans 11:29). On the other hand, a willing vessel can be used by the Holy Spirit to distribute all types of anointing's, and the list is without measure.

Just because the anointing was there at one time does not mean it will be there forever. There are special anointing's that are there for certain times and for a specific season. Anointing's are different from spiritual gifts; they can come and go, but the gift and calling will never leave you.

It is as though the angels are soaring around the populace of God's people, constantly seeking out the fragrance of Christ Jesus

His Anointed Fragrance of Knowledge

that has been released through any one of His people. As soon as the fragrance is released into the spiritual atmosphere, an angel immediately descends upon that person. This is when the anointing is activated.

It is just like when a flower gives off its aroma; bees and butterflies are drawn to it. They come to drink of its nectar, taking with them the collected seeds from the flower, pollinating all the other flowers that will receive the butterfly. Metaphorically this is you, the anointed one, as angels are drawn to you by the fragrance of Christ's Spirit in you.

"But you have an anointing from the Holy One, and you know all things" (1 John 2:20).

The anointing can lift, though. The anointing can change. People can shift from an evangelistic anointing to pastoral anointing, or from the prophetic to apostolic anointing. It can move from one of the five-fold ascension ministries to the next. It is like you are majoring in a specific degree in college with a minor in a different subject, yet both degrees complement each other for a specialized position or job. For instance, a tax-attorney is required to have a Law degree as well as a CPA degree. This same concept works in ministry.

However, you can be anointed for a time and season to operate in one of the ascension gift ministries or any one of the gifts of the Holy Spirit. Even Paul prophesied, but he was an apostle. Not all apostles prophesy, yet the gift can be there. The gifts and callings are irrevocable, but the anointing can change. We often fail to

127

recognize this, or we mistake the anointing for the gift or calling. The anointing comes from the unction or leading of the Holy Spirit.

If you hear what you think to be an anointed message, it is safe to say you've just been pollinated because you are being called into that type of calling or spiritual gifting. If the minister is delivering an anointed message, then the fragrance of the anointing is spreading the fragrance into those who are being called of God.

Ministering Without the Anointing

Many ministers are still ministering the way the Holy Spirit led them years ago, but today there is no longer any sign of the anointing in their ministry. They know that something is missing because the joy of ministering has left them. They should realize God has changed directions for them. They need to get under that anointed cloud, back under that pillar of fire and power so that they can find out what God wants to do through them.

As anointing's change, we must change because that is where He, the Anointed One, is. To be in an anointed place is to be safe, for you are under the covering of His Spirit. If we are under the guidance and direction of the Holy Spirit, then we will be in the perfect will of the Father.

As for Christians, it is a life-long challenge to find out what we are anointed to do. The anointing we receive from the Holy Spirit is different than the calling of God. Many men and women of God are called to preach or teach, but few receive the anointing to operate in the gifts of the Holy Spirit. It is the gift of the Holy Spirit that establishes your ministry. Apostle Paul said, "I long to see you, that I may impart to you some spiritual gift so that you may be established" (Rom. 1:11).

We are told in Luke 4:16–19 that our Lord and Savior went into the synagogue one day and read from the scriptures. In that moment, He read what He had been called to do for all mankind. Jesus was handed the book of the Prophet Isaiah, and He read it the way it is recorded in the New Testament, "The Spirit of the Lord is upon Me, because He has anointed Me to preach the gospel to the poor; he has sent Me to heal the brokenhearted, to proclaim liberty to the captives and recovery of sight to the blind, to set at liberty those who are oppressed; to proclaim the acceptable year of the Lord." Jesus knew what He was anointed to do and He fulfilled what His Father had sent Him to accomplish.

When His Word comes to you by a spoken word, through the written word, or even on a billboard as you are driving down the road, it is anointed of God and impossible to miss. Jesus was called and anointed to put an end to the curse of the law of sin and death. This is the way it happens for most of us, and when it does, you'll know without a doubt, for you will know that you know in your knower that God has an anointing for you.

Anointing's Change

The anointing is the unction of the Holy Spirit that is directing you into God's will for your life in that moment, hour, or season. There are times we need a new and fresh anointing to work in our lives because the old no longer works. The work of God is not to be mocked or taken lightly, for your anointing can turn from a wonderful fragrance from God to a horrible stench and the people will spiritually sense it.

"Dead flies putrefy the perfumer's ointment, and cause it to give off a foul odor; so does a little folly to one respected for wisdom and honor" (Eccles. 10:1).

Unfortunately, too many people keep holding on to the old anointing and lose the fragrance that once brought God's presence into their lives. If this ever happens to you, you will need to seek Him with all that is within you. Start with where you were going when you received your anointing and track down where you went wrong. In almost every case, the error began with not doing what God said and it probably was a minor request.

The Spirit cries within to begin searching for a new and fresh anointing. This is needed in order to move under His protection and receive the guidance of the Holy Spirit. Only then will you be able to accomplish the things God wants to accomplish through you. He is faithful to bless you with a new and fresh anointing. As long as you are doing what God has called you to do, there will be peace and harmony. You will be satisfied. Nobody will be able to touch you, and your emotions will all be intact.

"Thanks be to God who always leads us in triumph in Christ, and through us diffuses the fragrance of His knowledge in every place" (2 Cor. 2:14).

Do Not Tarry, For It Will Not Last

When God starts to move us in a certain way, we want to look at it and size it up. Is it comfortable? Is this something I want to do? Is this something that lines up with my dreams?

Our dreams can become nightmares when we try to forge them into our lives when God has NOT called us to walk in them. There are a lot of people trying to live out their dreams, but what they are doing is living out their own humanistic carnal nature, absent of His anointing. They struggle through life, trusting their own reasoning and rejecting God's revelation, all the while proclaiming, "We know that all things work together for good to those who love God, to those who are the called according to His purpose" (Rom. 8:28).

The problem is they are not in His purpose. If they had the anointing from the Anointed One they would not be banging their head up against the wall, confused, broken, and void of understanding as to why God isn't helping them. Believe me when I say His Kingdom is not like Burger King. I mean it, you can't get it whatever way you want it. You must pray (ask), hear (His voice), and Obey (exactly His way).

Knowing His True Anointing

We need to seek God's revelation for our lives. It does not matter if it doesn't manifest the way we think it ought too. What is important is that we are doing God's will and that can only be accomplished by His anointing.

Not everything that is drawing a crowd is anointed of God. For example, most people think that if they are rich then God has blessed them and anointed them to prosper, but we know this is not always true. You cannot measure your spirituality by how much money you have in the bank or even how poor you are. Wealth and popularity are not the measuring rods to measure God's anointing.

People build lots of things that are not of God. We see this all over the place. People may like the character of an individual or their personality or looks. They may like the way a person sings or speaks, or even the way they wear their hair. People are attracted to them because of the lust of the flesh and the pride of this life, but those that are born-again should not follow these worldly temptations. We cannot allow ourselves to be led by our fleshly emotions; we must be led by the anointing from the Holy Spirit.

"For all that is in the world—the lust of the flesh, the lust of the eyes, and the pride of life—is not of the Father but is of the world" (1 John 2:16).

Instead, we need to look at the anointing that rests upon the person. We have to ask ourselves if it is just entertainment or the anointing. It is sometimes hard to see the difference between being entertained and being taught something of value by the anointing of Christ. We need to know if it is our emotions that we are being moved by or if it is the Holy Spirit teaching us the ways and thoughts of God. The anointing teaches us all things, and it comes to us through the anointing that is given to men and women, as directed by the Holy Spirit.

"But the anointing which you have received from Him abides in you, and you do not need that anyone teach you; but as the same anointing teaches you concerning all things, and is true, and is not a lie, and just as it has taught you, you will abide in Him" (1 John 2:27).

Anointing vs. Emotions

It is with the anointing that we will identify our calling and His spiritual gift in our life, not in the emotions of the "flash in the pan" hype of the worldly. Jonathan Edwards delivered the sermon, "Sinners in the Hands of an Angry God," a classic of early American literature, during a revival in 1741.

In his bland monotone voice, he read his sermon about Hell, Heaven, and the God of wrath to a large crowd of early revivalists in America's first Great Awakening. As he began to read, people started to weep, faint, and scream. Over a short period of time, thousands became believers. It was the anointing—not hype—that birthed this revival. All Edwards did was stand up and read. The anointing drew the people into a vision of Hell as they experienced themselves being lowered into the fiery pit.

I have read the sermon, but I did not experience any of these things, nor did anyone else who I have read it to. Why? Because Jonathan Edwards was anointed for that time to be used of God to become a part of that Great Awakening, and the people knew it was all God.

If you ever read his sermon, you will wonder how it had an effect on so many people, but the anointing was there at that particular time. It does not mean that this is the way we all should do it. There are too many copycats. People try to copy someone else's anointing, but it just doesn't work. We need to find our own anointed message that God has put in our heart to share. There may be a likeness in the spirit of the same message others are preaching, but you still must have your own personal anointing that will touch those whom God has chosen.

In charismatic circles, anointings are revealed in powerful healing ministries, powerful sermons, and in the working of miracles, but there are also anointings in jobs. There are anointings in businesses. There are various anointings that help identify a person's calling and gifting. The anointing is what equips us and empowers us to build God's kingdom on Earth. He is using this world as part of His manufacturing process; it is used as a symbol, a shadow of things to come. The most important thing is to find out what you are anointed to do.

"To them it was revealed that, not to themselves, but to us they were ministering the things which now have been reported to you through those who have preached the gospel to you by the Holy Spirit sent from Heaven—things which angels desire to look into" (1 Pet. 1:12).

Quenching the Spirit

Everyone assumes they can tell the difference between an angel of the Lord and a fallen angel of Satan. I have found that it is easy to miss the presence of the angelic host of God. When they go unnoticed they depart, leaving you without direction. We are led by the Holy Spirit, as He appoints His angels (ministering spirits) to direct us. In order to properly discern the will of God, you must be very sensitive to the ministering spirits appointed to you. If you provoke one of these appointed angels, you can leave yourself wide open for a demonic attack.

"Behold, I send an Angel before you to keep you in the way and to bring you into the place which I have prepared. Beware of Him and obey His voice; do not provoke Him, for He will not pardon your transgressions; for my name is in Him. But if you indeed obey His voice and do all that I speak, then I will be an enemy to your enemies and an adversary to your adversaries" (Exod. 23:20–22).

God will never leave you nor forsake you, but you can quench the Holy Spirit, causing Him to withdraw His protective angels. When ministering, it is very important not to quench the Spirit. I cannot express the importance of how careful you must be not to transgress the ministering spirits that are appointed to minister for you. It is a frightening thing to stand before a group of people telling them you are going to hear God for them, and then the spirit of prophecy not be there for you.

"And I fell at his feet to worship him (the angel). But he said to me, 'See that you do not do that! I am your fellow servant, and of your brethren who have the testimony of Jesus. Worship God! For the testimony of Jesus is the spirit of prophecy'" (Rev. 19:10).

Many have interpreted this scripture in different ways. I will share with you what the Holy Spirit said to me in regards to its meaning. In the last line it says, "For the testimony of Jesus is the spirit of prophecy." The Holy Spirit said to me, "It is not one's personal testimony that is the spirit of prophecy; but the spirit of prophecy is the testimony revealing that Jesus is not dead but alive because He is speaking to you." Through the prophetic gifts we know many things about Him and what He is revealing about each one of us.

It only takes one blasphemous word or deed to cause the spirits of our Heavenly Father to leave you vulnerable to satanic attacks. Not only do you have to mind your manners in the presence of the ministering spirits, but the people must be in line with His desires as well. Keep watch over your thoughts or deeds, otherwise the spirits of our Heavenly Father will leave you high and dry.

"Furthermore, we have had human fathers who corrected us, and we paid them respect. Shall we not much more readily be in subjection to the Father of spirits and live?" (Hebrews 12:9).

I recall back in early 1995, I was ministering in a church of about 250 good ole country folks. During those days, I did not know that the Lord would show you whom to call out of a crowd to receive a word of prophecy, so I would just have everyone in the building that wanted a word form a single line at the altar. I would minister until everyone who wanted a word had received one. This could take hours! The longest period of time I have ministered non-stop is five and a half hours. That's without any kind of break at all; no water, no sitting down, and no stopping. With the supernatural strength of the ministering spirits, you do not have any physical needs; you are caught up in the realm of the spirit.

Now, after I had delivered my sermon I asked the people in this little country church to line up if they wanted a word from God. I did not really think many would believe I could hear God for them, because none of them had even heard of me. To my surprise, everyone in the building that I could see jumped into formation ready to receive.

After ministering to the first hundred or so, from the corner of my eye I saw a bright light flash by and depart from the sanctuary. I stopped ministering and turned to the pastor and elders who were standing right behind me. I said, "Someone has grieved the Holy

Spirit and the spirit of prophecy has left the building. I cannot minister anymore here today. I am sorry."

The crowd was confused and the pastor and elders began questioning me about what had happened. I told them that the last person I had ministered to had caused the angel to depart. They said, "It couldn't have been this person. He is very sensitive to the Holy Spirit. It had to be the person you ministered to right before him because she is not living right." I knew who had offended the messenger of God and it was not the person who the pastor and elders thought it was.

Six months later, I received a call from the pastor and he had a report for me. He reported that last Sunday morning the person I had said offended the angel of the Lord came before the congregation. He confessed he had believed my ministry was not of God and asked the people for forgiveness for being wrong. Since then I have ministered to that same congregation more than ten times, and our Lord has given life-changing prophetic words. To this day many of the people have remained partners and a few have become very close friends.

The manifestation of the gifts of the Holy Spirit is a sign from God that He is alive and watching over us. You may have never thought of it this way. I learned this truth from the Holy Spirit.

Angels are ministering for us as we operate in these gifts. When you are slain in the spirit it can feel like someone physically pushed you down or clipped you from behind the knees. It is an angel of the Lord that is doing the work of the Holy Spirit.

Have you noticed that some ministers demonstrate more of the gifts in their ministry than others? The reason is that they have more angels appointed to them than some of the other ministers. When ministering you begin to recognize the different presence of the various angels. This is one way we know what gift the Holy Spirit will have you to operate in next.

The presence of the ministering spirit that slays people in the Holy Ghost is different from that of the ministering spirit that brings the gift of healing. There are various gifts and ministry functions imparted by God and are appointed to different people.

"And God has appointed these in the church: first apostles, second prophets, third teachers, after that miracles, then gifts of healings, helps, administrations, varieties of tongues" (1 Cor. 12:28).

There are angels that have different powers over disease and sickness, just as Gabriel had different powers than Michael, the arch angel. I have seen people get frustrated and turn from using the gift God has given them because they did not understand this valuable revelation. At times they would pray for the sick and they would be healed, while other times they would not. Out of frustration, they gave it up altogether. A lot of the time, the reason why some were healed and others were not is because their ministering spirit only had power over certain illnesses, afflictions, or infirmities.

We are to perfect the gift by using it until we find out the measure of its power. We are given to minister God's love through His saving grace. What power does the ministering spirit have that is appointed to you?

To experience the accuracy of any gift, you must first find out what your calling is all about. When you know your calling, and you begin following its course, then you can focus on your gift. Most people want to just move in their gift but do not have a clue as to what they are called to do. If you do not follow your calling, your angel is not obligated to minister for you, hence no manifestation of the gifts.

Your calling may be evangelism, teaching, faith, hearing God, feeding the poor, helping orphanages or visiting prisoners. Whatever you are called of God to do, He is faithful to endorse it by signs and wonders following after you. However, if we are not willing to do what God has called us to do, His angels will not minister for us. Once you have clarity of what your calling is then do it and stick with it; in doing so you will experience the continual flow of the gifts.

When dealing with the prophetic, angels are vital parts in seeing the word delivered with power. Angels are sent to signify and clarify what God's purpose is for His people and to witness to the lost and uninformed people.

The book of Revelation was given to John by an angel. Prophets of today cannot deny that prophecy, words of knowledge, and words of wisdom are given to them in part by angels. To deny that His angels are speaking to us today would be to say that the Holy Scriptures are a lie.

"The Revelation of Jesus Christ, which God gave Him to show His servants; things which must shortly take place. And He sent and signified it by His angel to His servant John, who bore witness to the word of God, and to the testimony of Jesus Christ, to all things that he saw. Blessed is he who reads and those who hear the words of this prophecy, and keep those things which are written in it; for the time is near" (Rev. 1:1–3).

"Then he (the angel) said to me, 'These words are faithful and true.' And the Lord God of the holy prophets sent His angel to show His servants the things which must shortly take place" (Rev. 22:6).

"I, Jesus, have sent my angel to testify to you these things in the churches. I am the Root and the Offspring of David, the Bright and Morning Star" (Rev. 22:16).

Chapter 8

Molded by Trials and Tribulations

In Numbers Chapter 20, Moses disobeyed God's instructions and struck a rock rather than speak to it. One time before that, when the people needed water, God had Moses strike the rock. When he did, water from the dry rock appeared. However, this time God told Moses to SPEAK to the rock. Moses did not speak to it, but struck the rock like before. Over and over again, Moses struck the rock. Water eventually came out of the rock; however, God was angry with Moses for not obeying His command. Because of Moses' disobedience, God was not going to let Moses and the Israelites move one more inch. They were going to stay right there until they learned a hard lesson for Moses' disobedience.

They were trying to get to the Promise Land. However, the King of Edom would not let them go through his land and threatened to kill them if they tried. Moses tried to negotiate with the

King: he promised not to drink the water, and he said they would walk through the land instead of riding their beasts. They even swore to remove their shoes. They were willing to do whatever the king wanted, but the King of Edom refused their request.

Have you ever been in a place where God wouldn't let you leave or go where you needed to be? Every time you went into your place of prayer, nothing would happen, even though you prayed for days. It seemed like the heavens were closed. You couldn't get through. You couldn't hear God. Nothing was changing. Everything kept dishing out sorrow upon sorrow. There were only trials and tribulations.

You may have wondered how you were supposed to persevere through this and have endurance to grow in faith. Have you ever been in that place where all of a sudden you felt void of God's presence? You may question whether you are even saved. Have you ever experienced the feeling that you had messed up so badly that you were not ever going to make it out of the mess you had made? God does not want you to go any further until you deal with your disobedience to His word. God told you what to do and you did not do it.

Were you ever grounded from the things you loved to do because you didn't take out the trash like your parents asked? Your parents were not going to let you go anywhere until the trash was taken out, but you couldn't understand why it was such a big deal. It is not any different with our Heavenly Father. He wants you to do what He wants you to do and He wants you to do it the way He said to do it. We are talking about hearing God, but also obeying His every word.

If you are hearing God but not doing what He is saying to do, you will find yourself suffering for stepping out of His will.

Pray, Hear, and Obey, For It's the Christian Way

It is much easier to hear God for others and give them the words He wants said than it is to find God for yourself. When you are trying to hear God for yourself in the midst of a difficult situation, your emotions seem to be screaming at you, and when all your concerns are hollering it is very difficult to find out what you need to do. This is a similar situation Moses and Aaron found themselves in. They were thinking, "What are we going to do now? We can't get through Edom. Let us go back to the tabernacle and fall on our faces and see what God has to say."

It doesn't say how long they prayed, but when they went back, this is what the Lord had to say, "I want you to take Aaron and set him up at Mount Hor, strip him naked, and leave him for dead."

The Levitical law tells us that we are purged of our sins by putting an animal up for sacrifice. It doesn't say anything about a brother. When did it come about that we are supposed to leave a brother, a human being, as a sacrifice? Nowhere in the Levitical law did it say to do this, but it is what God was telling them to do. They had to pay the price before the people could go on, and the price was Aaron's life. The Lord said to take Aaron and put him on the mountain, strip him, put his clothes on his son, and leave Aaron there to die. So that is what they did. Aaron paid the price.

Do you see the prophetic story in that? Aaron paid the price for Moses' disobedience just as Jesus Christ has paid for all the many times you and I have disobeyed the voice of God. At some point, each and every one of us has disobeyed God's direct word, but the punishment has already been paid. Jesus has been made a sacrifice for all of us. Out of our disobedience we have been made obedient through what Jesus has done for us.

Aaron is an Old Testament symbol, a shadow of Christ. Aaron was placed on the hill and left for dead. The Israelites were then able to go on, but they had to go around Edom. God's word and Aaron's sacrifice gave them clearance to get around Edom. They would not have moved forward until Aaron was offered up as a sacrifice for Moses' sin against God, the sin of being disobedient to God's command.

God told Moses in Egypt that He would give him Aaron to be his spokesman. God said in Exodus 4:14–16, "Is not Aaron the Levite your brother? I know that he can speak well. And look, he is also coming out to meet you. When he sees you, he will be glad in his heart. Now you shall speak to him and put the words in his mouth. And I will be with your mouth and with his mouth, and I will teach you what you shall do. So he shall be your spokesman to the people. And he himself shall be as a mouth for you, and you shall be to him as God."

Aaron was the prophet and voice for Moses. Aaron vocalized whatever he heard Moses say. Aaron was also the sacrifice that allowed his people to move forward. Aaron was the type and shadow of the one to come,

"And the Lord spoke to Moses and Aaron in Mount Hor by the border of the land of Edom, saying: 'Aaron shall be gathered to his people, for he shall not enter the land which I have given to the children of Israel, because you rebelled against my word at the water of Meribah'" (Num. 20:23–24).

We cannot just do whatever we want and expect God's blessing to always be with us. Grace abounds until our disobedience causes grace to run out. Understand what the Lord is teaching us through this tragic story of Aaron's death. Those of you who are in ministry must know from experience that the closer you get to the Lord, the quicker God's judgment comes.

Those of us in ministry suffer severe judgment for leading His people astray through incorrect actions or teachings. What you used to get away with before you started hearing God's voice you will no longer be able to get away with as you grow in the Lord. Lessons in life will quickly teach you that He is serious, so do not make the mistake of taking His word as an option. The positive side of this is that you will learn more about His ways and thoughts and how He sees His Church today. At all cost, stay away from the things that anger God the most! Disobedience is at the top of His list.

I Am a Witness

My brother-in-law, Wes, was the praise and worship leader when his pastor decided to move to another state. The pastor wanted Wes to take over as pastor of the church. He did not want to do that because his father had been a pastor and Wes had watched his father go through some very hard times.

However, Wes finally surrendered and accepted the position. The following day, the pastor received an offer on his house which he had been trying to sell for over a year. At the same time, Wes experienced a breakthrough. You see, Wes was in business with his brother Steven; they were buying and fixing up homes to sell, but the homes were not selling. They tried everything they knew to sell these properties. They put up banners and contracted the specialized services of different realtors, but nothing good was coming of it. Only more debt.

Wes decided to accept the pastoral position, and right after he did everything started to change. Within a couple of weeks, the homes which were a heavy financial burden to the brothers were sold. Because of this, Wes was a changed person. He was truly blessed after yielding and moving into the very position he had tried to avoid. When we are in God's will the devil cannot touch us. Everything changes when we decide to die to our desires and follow Jesus.

"We know that whoever is born of God does not sin; but he who has been born of God keeps himself, and the wicked one does not touch him" (1 John 5:18).

The Abundant Life

"And the disciples came and said to Him, 'Why do you speak to them in parables?' He answered and said to them, 'Because it has been given to you to know the mysteries of the kingdom of Heaven, but to them it has not been given'" (Matt. 13:10–11).

Unbelievers cannot understand us, for they only have the knowledge of this world. They do not know where we are coming from or what is going on within us. All they see is the outer shell. They think we have lost our minds, or are just stupid.

We know we are peculiar in the name of Christ. We have a life that they could only hope for. It is only by the grace of God that we have what we have. It was by His choice that He chose us and we received Him as our Lord and Savior.

There are people who reject eternal life and choose to only live the way of the world. They rejected the conviction of the Holy Spirit and have found themselves miserable, though some have returned, crying out to God to receive them. When that door opens, you had better go through it right away. You do not choose when to be born-again; that choice is God's. It is only when God opens the door for you that you can truly come in.

But when God closes the door, no man can open it for you. When you feel the conviction of the Holy Spirit upon you, you cannot afford to reject His calling. Many have lived a lukewarm life for Christ, denying Him full control of their life, thus losing in the exchange His gift of eternal life. "So then, because you are lukewarm, and neither cold nor hot, I will vomit you out of my mouth" (Rev. 3:16).

"Then He said to them, 'Take heed what you hear. With the same measure you use, it will be measured to you; and to you who hear, more will be given. For whoever has, to him more will be given; but whoever does not have, even what he has will be taken away from him'" (Mark 4:24–25).

This verse is talking about the mysteries of the Kingdom of Heaven. Jesus said, when you pray, go to the Father in reverence, and when you receive the revelation from Heaven and act upon it you will have the abundant life. Many people refer to the abundant life spoken of in the book of Acts, but they do not have an abundant life. They don't understand why Satan has entered into their lives to steal, kill, and destroy them. They question why these things happen to them, but do not understand that it is because there is a lack of obedience.

The Key is Obedience

If you will crucify your flesh and not reason it within your soul, you will have the abundance and God will continue to bless you over and over again.

Obedience requires self-humiliation and humbling yourself to Christ in order for the obedience to actually work in your life. When Jesus asks you to do something, you may fight it within yourself. There is a warring between the flesh and the spirit, but if you will crucify the flesh and not reason it within your soul (mind, will, and emotions), you will have the abundance of God and He will continue to bless you over and over again. Don't weigh it out, just do it.

"Therefore I speak to them in parables, because seeing they do not see, and hearing they do not hear, nor do they understand. And in them the prophecy of Isaiah is fulfilled, which says: 'Hearing you will hear and shall not understand, and seeing you will see and not perceive; for the hearts of this people have grown dull. Their ears are hard of hearing, and their eyes they have closed, lest they should see with their eyes and hear with their ears, lest they should understand with their hearts and turn, so that I should heal them.' But blessed are your eyes for they see, and your ears for they hear" (Matt. 13:13–16).

This is not about the physical eyes and physical ears. This is about visions and hearing in the realm of the spirit, for that is where Christ lives. That is why the Lord prayed so much, to receive what God the Father wanted Him to do next.

Jesus waited four days before he went to the tomb of Lazarus. He could not go on the second or the third day because it wouldn't have worked. It had to be in God's timing. It had to be when God the Father said "Go."

Fish Bait Prophecy

There is only one case in the entire Bible where a given prophecy did not come to pass. In the book of Jonah, Jonah was sent by God to Nineveh to prophesy the destruction of their great city. However, when Jonah gave the word of the Lord, the King of Nineveh believed the word of the Lord and called for a fast. Then God saw their works and turned the evil away from them. God relented from the disaster that He had said He would bring upon them (Jonah 3:10).

This made Jonah angry with God and he began to sulk. The Lord said to him, "Are you feeling sorry for yourself because I did not kill 120,000 people and their livestock just so you could be right?" (See Jonah Chapter 4).

This is what we refer to in prophetic circles as being God's fish bait. He does not care if His prophets are always liked by all the people, for He is no respecter of persons. As long as His will is accomplished, He does not care how it gets done—even if it makes you look like a fool. To be used of God is not always to be used in the manner we choose. We can be used of God in many different ways, and not all of them are pleasing to our flesh.

Your Purpose, the Process, His Promise

When our Father's abiding word is working within you, you have found your purpose for your life, and this purpose becomes your identity. Too many believers today do not know where they fit in the Kingdom of God. One of the very first acts of every Christian should be to find out what God's purpose for them is in this life. Before we can begin to please God with our works we must first find out what His purpose is for us.

If we are not of this world, then we should not be so concerned about where we fit. This short time we have on Earth is a time of testing to see if we are loyal subjects who will serve our Father or serve the ruler of this world, the prince of darkness (see Ephesians 2:2). This life is training us to be prepared to endure the lengthy boot camp God has called us into.

Our Father has a three-part purpose for giving each and every one of us a word. It gives us direction on what we are called to do for His people. The word gives purpose by revealing to us how we are to go about fulfilling the work He has placed before us. He has a purpose for imparting into us a spiritual gift from the Holy Spirit so that we will be equipped to demonstrate His power, letting all know that we are His anointed ones for the job He has purposed us to do.

When most of us begin to think about what we could possibly do for the Kingdom of God, we are limited in our thoughts to just a few duties found within the local congregation. You might consider being a pastor, a praise and worship leader, a sound and technical person, a Sunday school teacher, or one of the other "smaller" positions. We cannot limit God and keep Him locked in the box that man has created, thinking these are the only expressions of His church the world will see. Our Father is much more radical than what most people may think, so do not be surprised if His word to you sounds a bit unethical and unacceptable to the religious standards many of the pious bunch hold today.

One of the most quoted verses of Scripture that most of us have either heard or been falsely corrected by is found in Romans 8:28, "And we know that all things work together for good to those who love God, to those who are called according to His purpose." If you read this verse a couple of times, you might see that there is a condition within this verse that is very important. It seems that every time things do not work out for one of our brothers or sisters, we quote this verse as to say it's okay. "You love God, however you are going to make mistakes, or bad things are going to happen to you and that's just the way it is."

Well, I have found that the part that makes all the difference is found in the last few words of this verse, "called according to His purpose." If you read this verse as it is written, you will see that it is saying that if you are in God's purpose and do all things according to His word (your calling, commission, and gifting) good things will come to you and the evil one cannot touch you.

Most people think that if they are doing good things for people then they are fulfilling God's purpose, but that is simply not so. I counsel people almost every day. Many of them are doing good things in the site of the religious bunch to impress one another, and God too. But their good deeds are dead works in the eyes of God, leaving them to be an open target for Satan to mess up their lives. Now, if they are doing what our Father has commissioned them to do then the devil cannot touch them; "he who has been born of God keeps himself, and the wicked one does not touch him" (1 John 5:18).

Or do you believe that God has no power over the devil? Let's get real here, God created ALL things, and this includes Satan who also has a purpose. Remember, "He comes to steal, kill, and destroy" (John 10:10). What is your purpose and what are you called, commissioned, and equipped to do for our Master and Lord Jesus Christ and His Church?

The Process, Baptism of Fire

There is a process that everyone must go through before they can receive their promise. No one likes the process and some fail the test by doubting God and His word. That is why the verse says, "For many are called, but few are chosen" (Matt. 22:14).

Not everyone is able to hold on to His word through all the obstacle courses this boot camp has laid out to test their faith. To be in God's army, you have to be fit to endure it all until you finally come to the place where all the pain and suffering just does not matter anymore. Many make grand commitments to the Holy Spirit while standing in the midst of His Shekinah glory. It is easy to serve God when you feel as though Jesus has His hand on your shoulder.

The real test comes when you are standing toe to toe with the devil and he is doing his best to get you to believe him rather than God, and beating you down with doubt and disbelief. Remember these words when you are being tested in this manner: He that is in you is greater than he that is of this world. Don't doubt in darkness what you have committed to in the light. Everything will be all right, for when you have passed through the process you will reap what has been promised to you.

Before David was placed upon the throne, he received a word from Prophet Samuel that he would, in fact, someday become the king (1 Sam. 16:1–13). Twenty years later, that word came to pass because David kept that word in his forethoughts. Every time he was challenged by whatever obstacles were thrown into his path, he was reminded of his purpose.

During the process, David's prophetic word was put to the test. When David faced Goliath and he took the five small stones to challenge the giant, it was nothing because his faith had grown to the point where he knew the giant could not touch him. David was believing in the word of God and fulfilling the purpose in his life.

He was also challenged many times when he faced Saul in the wilderness. David could have died, but his prophecy had not come to pass yet. Therefore, he could not die and he had power to escape Saul.

The evil one cannot touch you if you are in the will of God. If the devil is beating you up, then something is wrong. You need to find out from the Lord if He wants you to be somewhere else or if you need to change what you are doing. God is holding men and women accountable today in what they say and how they lead His troops into this new battle.

"My brethren, let not many of you become teachers, knowing that we shall receive a stricter judgment" (James 3:1).

There is greater accountability for those who are in leadership, because they are accountable to God Almighty for what they tell others to do. They are accountable for your soul. Being a leader is not a picnic or a party. The church is not another club to join. It is becoming an entity that is issuing fatigues and bars and stripes. It is calling out those who will fight in this spiritual war.

Remember, what you do in this life will determine your rank and position for eternity. How you lead others in this life will determine where you are placed in His chain of command. Don't let the devil give you an image of Heaven with you wearing a white gown while sitting on a cloud strumming a harp. That is not the Kingdom of Heaven!

Those who have gone to the other side, those who have died and returned, have said it is just like Earth but much, much better. Sometimes we take this life far too seriously. In all reality we are too comfortable. When we begin to concern ourselves with this life more than the one to come, our life becomes difficult to find peace or hear the Prince of Peace.

When you are called out by God and His word abides in you, you have chosen to come in agreement with His word. You have saluted and marched toward the call of God, and you cannot afford to look back. "But Jesus said to him, 'No one, having put his hand to the plow, and looking back, is fit for the kingdom of God'" (Luke 9:62).

Don't look to the past and lament about how things used to be. We do not serve a God of the past. He is a God of today. He is not a God who died, gave us a book, and put us in charge. God is ruling and reigning from Heaven now.

Every situation and every occurrence in your life has a meaning from Heaven above. In everything that happens in your life, there is a cause and effect. When unexpected things happen to you and you do not know why, you need to seek God and find out. You have a right to know and you can find out because Jesus is alive and speaking to everyone who will follow the sound of His voice.

His Promises Will Come to Pass IF . . .

The promises of God are very personal and are directly connected to your doing whatever He asks you to do. The more you do for Him, the more He will do for you. It is like any other relationship: you must be willing to give of yourself even at the most difficult of times. The devil will try and make you believe God just wants to take your life and make you a slave. Not so. In fact, you will find that after you have served Him awhile and have proven to Him you are loyal to do whatever He asks of you, He will trust you with more and more of His power, people, and resources. It is a great thing when you have finally come to the place where God starts calling you His friend. To be a friend of God is to operate in a higher covenant with Him; you find yourself in a relationship that is full of His promises.

Over the years I have witnessed people trying all kinds of weird methods in an attempt to force the promises written in the bible to come to pass for their needs. I have heard many preachers saying that we can have whatever we ask just by claiming it in the name of Jesus, as if you can use His name to cast spells. The bible is not like Aladdin's lamp. We cannot just rub it three times while chanting a few verses and receive whatever we are wishing for.

To have a true friend takes a lot of effort and years of bonding. With each battle you find yourself in, you know your Friend is always right behind you backing you up. You have to want to go the distance with Jesus in order to build this type of relationship. He desires us all to be His friend; that is what He created us for. Begin building your relationship with Jesus today by asking what you can do for Him rather than telling Him what YOU want. This is the KEY that unlocks the door to the abundant life He promised you and me.

God's Revelation Knowledge vs. Human Reasoning

When you have prayed to our Father and you know that you know in your "knower" that He has heard you, things begin to change. After God delivers you from the place you were trying to leave, He will close the door and you will find yourself waiting for the new door to open. We call this place the "hallway" and it is sometimes dark and scary in this spiritual hallway. You may want to bail, jump ship, or abandon God's plan.

When you are in the "hallway," you should not make any major decisions. You must wait until you see the light coming through the door that stands open for you, then move toward the light and trust God. If you will allow God to lead you then you will find out who you are in Him. The hour has definitely come; we are going to see major changes. God has a plan and He is getting us ready for something big.

A lot of people are proclaiming that everything is great, but when it all falls apart the people who rested on those words are going to be devastated. However, there are people who are preparing for it. It is important for us to stay out of debt and try to be as financially free as we possibly can. To be a poor man is a hard thing, but the worst thing is to be a poor man in debt. You may not have all the material things you desire, but at least you have zero debt. It is easier to find a morsel of spiritual bread, which is a word from God, than to keep looking every day for the stale loaf the world continues to promise.

"It is written, 'Man shall not live by bread alone, but by every word that proceeds from the mouth of God'" (Matt. 4:4).

For years we have heard that we need to stay out of debt, yet people have wondered why. They thought everything was getting better. We must know what God wants us to do in the financial arena in order to have foresight on what we need to do for future plans. We need 20/20 foresight, not 20/20 hindsight. The only way to do that is to be in touch with the Lord and to work under His anointing.

The time has come when God is telling certain people what to buy and sell, and when to sell and where to buy. God will begin to prosper us and take us through a time that will be very difficult. We cannot go on what the world promises; we must go with what the word of the Lord is for each and every transaction we make. He is the only bread we need. When we know what God wants us to do, then we will know peace. God's word will always test us. We are often being tested by His word; we either trust Him or trust the ways of this world.

"I am the bread of life. He who comes to me shall never hunger, and He who believes in me shall never thirst" (John 6:35).

Chapter 9

Your Appointed Angel

"Now it came to pass, in the morning watch, that the LORD looked down upon the army of the Egyptians through the pillar of fire and cloud, and He troubled the army of the Egyptians" (Exod. 14:24).

In this verse, our Lord is described as being a pillar of fire by day and a cloud by night. There are times while preaching that this same pillar of fire comes and anoints you with his power. Could it be an angel of the Lord gives us the power to preach the good news of Jesus Christ?

There is a connection between the anointing and the Angel of the Lord. Many say that the Angel of the Lord recorded in the Old Testament was Jesus Christ Himself. Old Testament references that capitalize the word "Angel" could be referring to Jesus Christ. At other times it is thought that Jesus appeared and spoke as a man (Gen. 18:2–22; 32:24–30; Josh. 5:13–15). Any reference that does not capitalize "angel" could be referring to one of the other angels of the Lord.

There are many passages in which the expression "Angel of God" is certainly used for a manifestation of God himself (Gen. 22:11; Exod. 3:2). Those who believe in Jesus Christ have His Spirit living within them; therefore, the same pillar of fire could manifest itself today through the indwelling of the Holy Spirit.

"And I fell at his feet to worship him. But he said to me, 'See that you do not do that! I am your fellow servant, and of your brethren who have the testimony of Jesus. Worship God! For the testimony of Jesus is the spirit of prophecy'" (Rev. 19:10).

The first time I preached and prophesied in a church was in February of 1988. After preaching under the anointing of the Lord, and prophesying in the spirit of prophecy, several people came to me to ask questions. One dear woman did not have a question, but rather wanted to share with me what she had heard and seen during the meeting. Now, this lady was by no means spiritually-minded, and she really doubted whether the gifts of the Holy Spirit were for today. When I saw her come towards me, I began to prepare myself for a good tongue-lashing.

To my surprise, she was crying and a bit shaken. I asked her what was wrong. She replied that while I was prophesying, the Lord spoke to her and gave her a sign. I was pleased to hear that she had heard the voice of the Lord! I was even more stunned, however, to hear what she had seen as a sign from God. This dear lady was told by the Lord to tell me that every word that was spoken was protected and that not one word would touch the ground. I was ready to do the Holy Ghost dance right then and there, but that was not all she had to say.

A sign of the Lord was shown to her while I was ministering. Every time I moved away from the pulpit, a bright light would blind her eyes until I stood still. She told me it appeared as if the light was hiding behind me. I believe this sign was given to her from God as her confirmation that she was to give me the word that He wanted me to hear. I did not know at that time how important that word would be to me later that day.

When I finally returned home and had lain down to rest, I felt the anointing leave me. As soon as the anointing left, the devil began whispering words of doubt and confusion. He told me I needed to get up and call various people I had prophesied over. He was telling me that the words I delivered were incorrect.

He continued to torment my thoughts, trying to convince me I had messed up someone's life and that they would perish because of what I had spoken over them. This went on for a few minutes. Then the Holy Spirit reminded me of the word I had received from the woman who had seen the blinding light. So I simply told the devil what the Lord had said, rebuked him, turned over, and took a little nap.

I experienced what Jesus promised would happen as soon as we deliver His word: the devil would try to steal it. "And He [Jesus] said, 'To you it has been given to know the mysteries of the kingdom of God, but to the rest it is given in parables, that seeing they may not see, and hearing they may not understand. Now the parable is this: The seed is the word of God; those by the way-side are the ones who hear; then the devil comes and takes away the word out of their hearts, lest they should believe and be saved'" (Luke 8:10–12).

I learned many things that day, but this one lesson I hope never to forget: whenever God gives you a word for someone and you are commanded to deliver it, the devil will try to steal it. It is by your faith that you delivered the word and it will be by your faith that the word will come to pass.

"Having then gifts differing according to the grace that is given to us, let us use them: if prophecy, let us prophesy in proportion to our faith" (Rom. 12:6).

The devil will try to get you to come into agreement with him that the prophecy you delivered was incorrect. If you come into agreement with the devil and his word, you will give the promise of God over to him, robbing the person of their prophecy and promise. Many nights I have resisted the devil as he has tried to steal the promise of the words delivered to the people through the gift that I received by the prophecy and the laying on of hands of the eldership.

A Massive Outpouring of Love and Power

God is sending His people spiritual gifts that are listed in 1 Corinthians 12, and also redemptive gifts that are listed in Romans

166

12. Another thing I have noticed is the variety of ministries being prophesied into existence are very unusual. These new ministries being birthed are nothing like anything we have ever seen before.

"There are diversities of gifts, but the same Spirit. There are differences of ministries, but the same Lord. And there are diversities of activities, but it is the same God who works all in all. But the manifestation of the Spirit is given to each one for the profit of all: for to one is given the word of wisdom through the Spirit, to another the word of knowledge through the same Spirit, to another faith by the same Spirit, to another gifts of healings by the same Spirit, to another the working of miracles, to another prophecy, to another discerning of spirits, to another different kinds of tongues, to another the interpretation of tongues. But one and the same Spirit works all these things, distributing to each one individually as He wills" (1 Cor. 12:4–11).

It is so obvious that the Holy Spirit is equipping the saints of God for a massive outpouring of God's love and power. More and more, I hear "brand name" preachers touch upon the need for angels. The connection between the angels, also known as ministering spirits, and the gifts of the Holy Spirit are coming more into focus. I was shown by the Holy Spirit a number of years ago about the variety of angels and how they effectively minister in various gifts of the Holy Spirit. You will be hearing more about this from other ministers as the days go by, for this revelation is huge and is sweeping across the nations.

If the Holy Spirit is tugging on your heart to seek a word of prophecy, it could be because He has a spiritual gift that He wants to impart into you to establish your ministry.

"For I long to see you, that I may impart to you some spiritual gift, so that you may be established" (Rom. 1:11).

"For the gifts and the calling of God are irrevocable" (Rom. 11:29).

Spiritual and redemptive gifts cannot ever be taken away from you. Be not foolish, however, with this newfound power from God for He is faithful to His Word and will not take the gift from you. However, if you harm His people or abuse them in any way, He will simply remove you.

"The fear of the LORD is the beginning of knowledge, but fools despise wisdom and instruction" (Prov. 1:7).

Angelic Enforcers of Spiritual Law

"I saw the Lord sitting on a throne, high and lifted up, and the train of His robe filled the temple. Above it stood seraphim; each one had six wings: with two he covered his face, with two he covered his feet, and with two he flew. And one cried to another and said, 'Holy, holy, holy is the Lord of hosts; the whole earth is full of His glory!'" (Isa. 6:1–3).

When the saints of the Lord come together to pray, praise, and worship, the angels will enter into the midst of them, making their presence known. This is when we begin to see people saved and the gifts of the Holy Spirit manifested. Angels are in our presence to deliver to the Father our confessions.

There are many spiritual laws that affect our lives, just as natural laws affect our physical world. We cannot see the law of gravity, but if we stand under a falling boulder we will feel its full effect. Spiritual laws, when misused, can have the same aftermath as the law of physics. It does not take faith to cause spiritual laws to manifest in our presence. The one thing that does differ is that spiritual laws are not controlled by time. The effects, good or bad, can come quickly or take years. On the other hand, nature's laws are time-controlled and are more easily understood. This is why it is hard for some Christians to understand why a heathen can seemingly go unpunished. However, scripture promises that judgment day will eventually come to all.

"Some men's sins are clearly evident, preceding them to judgment, but those of some men follow later. Likewise, the good works of some are clearly evident, and those that are otherwise cannot be hidden" (1 Tim. 5:24–25).

Another spiritual law that has a profound ability to return to its creator (like a boomerang) is the Law of Judgments. We begin to form judgments which affect our lives from day one. Judgments that we make in life can be good and return blessing back to us, or they can be bad and carry curses. We can make critical judgments of others and are guaranteed to receive the same in return. The criticism we receive usually comes from someone other than the person we have judged. It is also a law within the spirit realm that by the same measure of the infraction, we are guaranteed to have it come back on us in equal force or greater.

I will let you in on a little tidbit that will help you in prophesying, as well as in knowing of things to come. When you see a violation of God's spiritual law, you can then proclaim the outcome of the effects to that person or nation. This is how prophets are able to know of many things to come without even hearing God's voice. Now, what I have shared with you is very valuable information; however, there is one pitfall. If you witness someone breaking a spiritual law and you prophesy their punishment, know that if God grants them forgiveness, your words will fall to the ground and not come to pass.

Always keep this one spiritual law in your forethoughts before speaking evil about anyone. You are accountable for every word you speak. If you want to stand under the Master's gavel, then foolishly speak evil and you will experience firsthand the power of His wrath.

"Judge not, that you be not judged. For with what judgment you judge, you will be judged; and with the measure you use, it will be measured back to you" (Matt. 7:1–2).

The Spiritual Law of Giving

Something material for something spiritual is also a spiritual law that carries blessings and curses. In this law, we find that it is not "how much you give" but "who you give it to" that is important. You can give a psychic a twenty-dollar bill for a reading and receive a curse. On the other hand, you can give to God's ministers and be blessed.

Let us not stop there. We must also understand that this spiritual law is only in effect if the one ministering accepts your monetary gift. Apostle Paul goes into great length explaining to the saints in Corinth about this spiritual law. At the end of his message he robs them of their blessing by not accepting their offering. (See 1 Corinthians 9:1–18)

"Whoever goes to war at his own expense? Who plants a vineyard and does not eat of its fruit? Or who tends a flock and does not drink of the milk of the flock?" (1 Cor. 9:7).

The boundaries for giving that have been set by many Christians today do not line up with Scripture. In fact, there are a large number of Christians who believe that if you minister, you should do it without any monetary return. It appears that the church at Corinth, in Apostle Paul's day, had the same problem. This is why he goes into such great length to bring the church back in line with Scripture. He is saying that if one plants wheat, one should eat of that wheat. Or if he raises sheep, he should eat of its meat. Or if he has goats, he should drink of their milk.

It costs a lot of money to fight back the spirit of darkness. The cost of publishing, materials, postage, travelling, and internet expenses are tremendous. The last thing we need is to waste time and finances trying to convince Christians of this spiritual truth.

"Do I say these things as a mere man? Or does not the (spiritual) law say the same also? For it is written in the Law of Moses, 'You shall not muzzle an ox while it treads out the grain.' Is it oxen God is concerned about? Or does He say it altogether for our sakes? For our sakes, no doubt, this is written, that he who plows should plow in hope, and he who threshes in hope should be partaker of his hope" (1 Cor. 9:8–10).

You do not have to be a prophet (or spiritual) to understand this law of exchange. If you have an ox that labors to grind out the seed for your bread, would you keep all of the grain for yourself? No! Any halfway intelligent person would know if you do not share the seed of the grain with the oxen, he will starve to death. Then you would not have oxen to tread out the grain for you.

Unfortunately, even at the closing of the 20th century, we still have Christians who want to starve those who are grinding out the word and revelation of God. Without the bread of life, we will become spiritual beggars falling to the ground, dry and hungry for God and His word. It seems to be no problem for the majority of people to live under the monetary rule of exchange when it comes to receiving food, entertainment, and other Earthly pleasures. They think nothing of giving their hard-earned money for food, pills, or even a movie, but struggle when giving to the ministers of the gospel.

Some say they cannot trust the ministers with their money. Does this mean they can trust the grocer, the doctor, the lawyer, and everyone else but God's ministers? What a minister offers cannot always be seen in the same manner as what you brought home in a grocery bag or the pharmacist's bottle. Do not be fooled by what you cannot see, for what is spiritual is eternal and you cannot purchase it; you can only support it.

If you are being blessed by one minister, but give your tithes and offerings somewhere else, you are in a sense committing a spiritual crime. Over the years, I have heard of people sneaking off to hear another preacher, but they left all their tithes and offerings at their traditional church. I prayed about this and asked the Lord for wisdom and this was what He had to say. He put it to me this way: "Do you take from the shelf at K-Mart and then go pay Wal-Mart for the product because that is where you have shopped at the longest?" We see this happening all over the Body of Christ. As a result, some of God's oxen are being muzzled.

"If we have sown spiritual things for you, is it a great thing if we reap your material things? If others are partakers of this right over you, are we not even more? Nevertheless we have not used this right, but endure all things lest we hinder the gospel of Christ" (1 Cor. 9:11–12).

The Bible Does Not Stutter

Nowhere in the Bible does it say that you are to give all your tithes to one local church or ministry. What the Bible does say is to give unto God what is rightfully HIS! (See Malachi 3:8.) How do you do that? It is easy! If you are receiving revelation from God through a ministry or church, then you have found His Spirit and that is where He wants you to sow your tithes and offerings. Think about it: if God has chosen to speak to you through that person, do you suppose that this might be where He would want you to give of your material things? If the minister is good enough for God, how much more should we be willing to bless him/her?

"Do you not know that those who minister the holy things eat of the things of the temple, and those who serve at the altar partake of the offerings of the altar? Even so the Lord has commanded that those who preach the gospel should live from the gospel" (1 Cor. 9:13–14).

Here we find another commandment of the Lord that we can obey or disobey. If the Lord has commanded those who preach the gospel to live from the gospel, then we need to support those who labor in this good news. What could be the punishment for not taking care of those who are laboring for God's word?

Have you ever tried to find God after He has hidden Himself so well that you feel abandoned? The prophet Amos prophesied of a famine that would come. The famine would not be one of food or water but of the words of the Lord (Amos 8:11–12). I am sure there were still priests, prophets, and kings in that day, but God was not speaking through any of them. Why? Because the people had closed their hands, making a fist in the face of God. They would not give to His workers as commanded, so they were cursed.

"Will a man rob God? Yet you have robbed Me! But you say, 'In what way have we robbed You?' In tithes and offerings. You are cursed with a curse, for you have robbed Me, *even* this whole nation" (Mal. 3:8-9).

The day the Lord had me start asking people to give something of value for a prophecy seemed to be the same day that I started fighting my flesh and the devil. You see, I was proud and I did not want to be supported by God's people. It made me feel out of control to depend on the people for my needs. I would rather paint houses or work at the grocery store than take money for preaching and prophesying.

I have really experienced the power in this verse of scripture that says, "It is better to give than to receive." (See Acts 20:35.) Believe me, it is much easier to do physical labor and receive a regular paycheck than to earn your wages from spiritual labor. Once you have been humbled to depend upon the people for your livelihood, you realize that you have given up the freedom to do and say whatever you want. You become much more responsible to the people that God sends your way, and will find yourself praying much harder for their wealth, health, and sound mind.

These attacks are not our battles to fight because God defends his own. My wife and I have tried very hard to do only what God has told us to do, and that is not always what others want us to do. I asked the Lord over and over again, "Why do we have to ask the people to give in order to receive?" He has responded many ways, but each time He has not wavered in His reasoning.

He once said, "Son, the gospel is not free; it cost me my life!" Another time He responded to my plea with these words: "Son, if they have nothing invested in the word they receive, it will be worthless to them." On another occasion the Lord said, "The gospel is not free; it will cost you this life in exchange for life eternal."

One time when I became very stressed over finances, the Lord said to me, "Son, do not take this life too seriously, for this is not it!" After hearing the Lord's words so many times, I have learned to become very firm in the way we handle things in this ministry, for it is His ministry we are entrusted with. Now when we receive hate mail or rebukes for asking for financial support, it just makes me more determined to preach the truth about the spiritual law of giving and receiving.

In the exchange of spiritual things for monetary gifts, the devil has worked overtime on a large portion of God's people. The fact is, the Bible is not a book of lies. It fully supports the spiritual law of exchange, although we need to make sure that we are supporting the church or ministry that is producing God's word and blessings. To give just to be giving does not always produce God's rewards and blessing.

Angels Perform the Will of the Holy Spirit

The Holy Spirit is the presiding ruler of God's Kingdom on Earth and is making judgments daily about who will be rewarded and who will not. If He can trust you to give when He sends an angel of the Lord (who prompts you to give), then He is faithful to reward you. However, if you have the unction of the Holy Spirit come upon you to give, and you reason away why you shouldn't give, then the Holy Spirit cannot trust you.

You cannot expect Him to bless you just because you have people praying in agreement with you or claiming promises from the Holy Scripture. Blessings only come by the grace of God and your obedience to His desires. The Bible is not some book of incantations where you can just chant whatever you want and expect the Holy Spirit to hop up and down and do whatever you say. No! You must establish a relationship with Him that is based upon your doing whatever the Holy Spirit asks of you, before you can expect Him to do something for you.

The spiritual laws of exchange go much deeper than just memorizing a few scriptures from the Bible. You can't quote a verse and believe for the promise to come your way if you are unwilling to obey the Holy Spirit's request.

It might sound odd to you, but the Holy Spirit will even use a heathen to give if He cannot find a loyal believer. That is why you see the Spiritual Law of Exchange working even for those who do not regularly attend church or mention God's name with praises upon their lips. Even a heathen can admit when he has been graced with a gut feeling, a hunch, or just something inside that told him to give, and he did it. He will say, "Here I am, a blessed man." Pray, Hear, and Obey! It is the only way to have the blessing of the Lord move in your life.

"Now it shall come to pass, if you diligently obey the voice of the Lord your God, to observe carefully all His commandments which I command you today, that the Lord your God will set you high above all nations of the earth. And all these blessings shall come upon you and overtake you, because you obey the voice of the Lord your God" (Deut. 28:1–2).

Chapter 10

God's Prophets and His Angels

"**M**y brethren, take the prophets, who spoke in the name of the Lord, as an example of suffering and patience" (James 5:10).

Walking in the office of the prophet is not all bad. It does have its high points. As long as you stay dedicated to seeking God, controlling your emotions and personal thoughts, you will be found to be a useful instrument of God for His people.

The life blood of any caring prophet is the testimonies cataloged in their ministry portfolio. Without the continual positive reports coming in from the people of God, you feel the prophetic stream within drying up, leaving you a parched and lonely vessel. However, each report confirming that you have heard God clearly brings a new and fresh anointing, giving you the boldness to go deeper when seeking God for the next batch of requests.

"He who receives a prophet in the name of a prophet shall receive a prophet's reward" (Matt. 10:41a).

We all agree that Jesus was and always will be "The Prophet." There are Major and Minor Prophets, but Jesus is "The Prophet," the ultimate Word of God. Therefore, this verse to me would make more sense if the Scripture read: He who receives a prophet in the name of "The Prophet" (referring to Jesus), rather than "a prophet in the name of a prophet." To receive a word from a prophet that came from "The Prophet," Christ Jesus, the King of kings and Lord of lords, would be easier to understand. Wouldn't a reward mean much more to you if the reward came from The Prophet (Jesus), not just any old prophet?

"Believe in the Lord your God, and you shall be established; believe His prophets, and you shall prosper" (2 Chron. 20:20b).

Another reason to receive prophets in the name of "The Prophet" is the reward of prosperity. The word prosperity is defined as "help along the journey." There will be many times in life's travels that you will need a prophet to help you find your way back into the flowing grace of God's prosperity. We all know how easy it is to get off track and lose sight of where we are headed. That is another reason why God has given His Church prophets.

"And God has appointed these in the church: first apostles, second prophets, third teachers, after that miracles, then gifts of healings, helps, administrations, varieties of tongues" (1 Cor. 12:28).

Over the years, I have found it very difficult to work in the local church as a prophet. I have tried the five-fold ministry, three-fold ministry, and a few other formulas, but none seemed to work. The problems were always the same. The pastor or someone with a dynamic personality would take control, limiting what you could and couldn't say when giving a prophetic word, thereby taking over the Holy Spirit's job. The Bible calls this type of a prophet a hireling: one who is paid to speak on behalf of their employer and not their creator.

Or another popular personality, "The Jealous One," would always seem to rise to the occasion. This would be a person who felt they were not receiving enough attention, and as a result they would vow to do everything they could to run the prophet out of the congregation.

Finally, after much prayer and seeking Him for answers, the Lord gave me the reason why this was not working out in the local body of believers. It was not about the format of five-fold or three-fold, but the answer was found in the true understanding of what the Church is supposed to be rather than what we have made it to be.

Over the years, our daily language has painted a picture of what we think the church is. For instance, "I got saved and began to go to church." Another cliché is: "What church do you belong to?" There are countless others, but the fact is there is only one Church, and it is neither a denomination nor non-denomination. The people of God are the Church and the Kingdom of God on Earth.

When I study the Old Testament prophets of God, they were never found in the temples or synagogues. The prophets were far away from the crowd and were seeking the face of God. When the people saw the prophet or prophets of God coming down from the high places, they were all ears to hear what God was now saying.

Another thing I've learned is that when you are with the fellowship of the local body of believers and someone needs a word from God, and you are asked to give them a word, you will discover your prophetic word has no power. Why? The reason is two-fold.

First, if you are the prophet of the house of God, you will have to sort out if what you are hearing is from God or if it is something you already know about the person. You begin to question yourself, asking "Is this something I overheard or is my personal knowledge of the person influencing my words?" The second part is the recipient of the word will question in their mind if someone told the prophet about their personal life or about the problem they were experiencing. Both of these drastically diminish the power of the word, and there will be doubt and disbelief written all over it.

However, if the prophet is a total stranger ministering in the house of God, you would know right away if they were hearing God because they would not know if the things they were speaking were true or not. This is another reason why standing alone as a prophet of God is important for the people. The sacrifice is sometimes hard, but it's well worth the reward in knowing that you are truly helping His people by accurately hearing the pure and clear word from God.

"A prophet is not without honor except in his own country, among his own relatives, and in his own house" (Mark 6:4).

Learning by the Example of Others

I had no idea what to do when I was called into ministry in July of 1976, when the Lord spoke to me from Ezekiel 33. At the very end of the chapter there is a reference to being a prophet. According to my limited knowledge at that time, I thought prophets were men who wore camel skin coats and had honey dripping from their beards. I thought prophets must be weird people, but I really didn't know for sure because I did not know any at that time in my life. A few years after that, the Holy Spirit commissioned me. He revealed that I was to perform my duties by sending out prophesies through the mail.

After receiving my call to be a prophet of God, I felt the pressure of His hand start to move me toward learning the prophetic ministry, but I was not interested. I liked my job as bank president. Being highly respected in the community, my hours were great and I had something everyone wanted: money to loan. God wanted to humble me by making me look like a freak in the eyes of the people. I knew that my life in the spotlight would be over if I followed Him into this new way of living.

Some, like myself, do not have a choice when called into the ministry. They are going, either easily by listening and obeying, or through turbulent resistance. Believe me, if you resist, you will find out what it is like to live in the belly of a whale. It stinks, so please do not choose the hard way.

After the rug was jerked out from under me and the dust had settled, I diligently started pursuing the way of a prophet. I tried to enroll in various bible colleges, but God would not have it. I was confused and frustrated. Little did I know that the Holy Spirit would teach me what it really meant to be a prophet, all my duties and the ins and outs of the office of a prophet. I thought maybe a prophet was some old guy who got into peoples' faces, chewed them up one side and spit them out the other. I soon learned that is not what a true prophet of God is called to do.

Birthing of the Prophetic Gift

"Do not neglect the gift that is in you, which was given to you by prophecy with the laying on of the hands of the eldership" (1 Tim. 4:14).

In the spring of 1989, I was traveling with two seasoned apostles and a pastor who was thinking about starting a traveling ministry. We were going from one local body of believers to another in the western part of Texas. Being that I was the newest of the group, I was allowed to hold an early morning Bible study. This was not always well-attended being it was early and no one knew anything about me. I was still trying to find out who I was myself, and seeking God for answers about what kind of ministry He had for me.

We had been on the road for a few days when we met up with Dr. Bill Hammond's group of ministers. Ironically, it was in the same town where I was born: Big Spring, Texas. As we started the regularly scheduled services, I brought the early morning message, then the traveling pastor delivered his. The hosting pastor of the church decided that we would all meet up for lunch. I was honored to break bread with these men and to hear them discuss our plans for the afternoon and evening services. It was decided that Prophet Gary Brooks would be holding the evening service and that one of the apostles would minister the word in the afternoon.

That night Prophet Brooks delivered a wonderful message on imparting spiritual gifts through prophecy and the laying on of hands according to 1 Timothy 4:14. I was moved by the Holy Spirit to ask Prophet Brooks if he would lay hands on me and prophesy and see what gift the Holy Spirit had for me. Prophet Brooks replied that he could not do this unless the Holy Spirit instructed him to do so. I told him I understood and we went our separate ways.

The next day we began the same schedule as the day before. When the evening service came around, Prophet Brooks brought another strong, anointed message; however, right in the middle of his message he stopped and paused for a moment. Then he called me up to the front of the people and explained what he was about to do. He laid hands on me and began to prophesy, speaking of the gift of prophecy and positions I would hold in the Kingdom of God. Well, I did not fall out under the power of the Holy Spirit; in fact, I felt absolutely nothing. When I returned back to the home where I was staying for the night, I began questioning God if this impartation thing was even real.

The next morning, I woke up and began my morning prayer. Suddenly, I began to hear this voice telling me what to expect for the day and what I was to preach on. I abruptly interrupted and said, "I don't know who you are, but I will test you according to 1 John 4:1–2 and see if you are of God." I was a little shaken as I got ready and started toward the meeting where I was to join the other ministers to discuss the plans for the next service.

As the meetings progressed we decided we would hold a joint service in Midland, Texas. It was well-attended, and Prophet Gary Brooks was ministering one night. When the teaching portion of that service was over, Prophet Brooks announced that anyone wanting to receive a word from God should come forward. Well over 400 people gathered around the altar, not counting the children. We knew this was going to be an all-night service.

Prophet Brooks began to prophesy over each person, so I retreated to the back of the sanctuary. As I leaned against the door frame of the main entry, a man with his son of about 9 years in age stood next to me. The little boy who was standing in front of his Dad turned around and asked, "Daddy can I get a word from

God?" It was rather sad because the Dad knew that they would be waiting for hours before his son could receive his prophecy.

All of sudden the Holy Spirit spoke to me and said, "Are you going to allow me to use you as a vessel that I may speak through?" I answered the Holy Spirit saying, "If you want to use me have the father and little boy look at me." No more than having that thought, they both turned and stared at me. So I asked, "Does your boy want a word from God?"

The man knew that I was traveling with the group so he took me up on the offer. We found a room that was not occupied and I began to pray. Suddenly, that voice I had heard during my morning prayer began speaking a long dissertation of God's plans for the young boy. The youngster was my chance to put this voice to the test, so I began to say whatever I was hearing and experiencing. When I finished, the boy took off in search of a pen and paper to record the word.

Then the boy's dad walked over to a large set of double doors, and as he opened them you could see the altar and all of the people waiting for their chance to receive their prophecy. I was shocked when he began telling the overflow of people, "Come in here, this man can give you a word from God." With my eyes bulging in fear, I watched a flood of people start toward me, quickly forming a line. I had no idea that this man was the Associate Pastor.

I shared whatever I heard from this newfound voice. It was coming to me so fast that I had no time to really think. Some people would cry, others would chuckle, and a few just seemed stunned.

Of course, I had no idea if anything I was saying was correct, nor did I understand what the word was meaning to each person. I began to stop after I ministered to each person to ask them what the word meant to them. As each one explained, my faith began to rise and I felt much more confident in what I was doing.

I realized that I could trust this voice, but I wanted to know why it was so different. Many times I had heard the voice of God, but never had I heard Him this way. Until that day, He had never spoken in such great length, maybe a couple of sentences but no more. This voice was coming in like a machine gun.

Later, the Holy Spirit taught me the difference. What I learned was that when I received the gift of prophecy, an angel had been appointed unto me to minister for me, telling me whatever God wanted me to know about each person I spoke to. God had thrown me into the river knowing I would have to quickly learn to swim, and I have not stopped since that day.

The Key to Finding Your Purpose

When you finally submit to Him and vow to do whatever He wants you to do, His blessings will overtake you and bless you for years to come. If you hear God and obey, you cannot out-run His blessings. He will bless you in spite of yourself.

I was scared when God commissioned me to start offering my gift to the general public. I was to send out prophesies through the mail with no more information than a name and address. I had no idea where this would lead me. God promised that if I made myself available as a vessel for Him to speak through, He would bless me. He said wherever a prophecy was sent to, I would reap a harvest.

I was still reluctant to do it though, because nobody I knew was doing this type of ministry. The only thing that came close to working like this were the psychics and I did not want to be associated with that group. However, after three days of wrestling with what God wanted, I began to follow His command and make myself available as a vessel for Him to speak through.

Getting started is the Hardest Part

For me, the most difficult step in this path of ministry was when I sent out the first prophecy on an audio-cassette tape. I thought I would only do one or two of these requests; however, they have not slowed. From the time I started in November of 1989, I have sent out over 100,000 prophetic words. At one point, I had a tiny ad in Charisma Magazine. They immediately started receiving so much flak from other ministries and pastors that they wanted to cancel me.

God always gets what He wants. The ad continued in the magazine month after month for over five years. It was only later that I found out Charisma Magazine had anonymously requested personal prophesies for each of their office staff members. It was later reported to me that they were so touched by their individual prophecies that they unanimously decided they would NOT remove the ad from the magazine. God bless Charisma Magazine for standing up for what they believe!

Being Loyal to the Commission

When you act on what God has commissioned you to do there will be battles; but remember that they are His battles. Whatever you need, He will make sure you have it in order to complete the job. Just make sure you keep moving in the direction He wants. He will not leave you out in the middle of the desert without a supply line coming to assist you. He will not let you be caught off guard, nor allow your enemy to sneak up behind you and stab you in the back. You cannot afford to go another day without crying out to God and telling Him you will do what He asks of you.

When I started mailing out prophecies, it seemed like a foolish thing to do. It was very humbling when I was asked what kind of work I did. In the beginning, there seemed to be nothing to gain from doing what God asked. However, God will go to great lengths to change the hearts of the people.

A Prophet is Not without Honor, Except . . .

"God has appointed these in the church: first apostles, second prophets, third teachers, after that miracles, then gifts of healings, helps, administrations, varieties of tongues" (1 Cor. 12:28).

Where does it say in the Bible that these ministries and spiritual gifts — apostles, prophets, and teachers — were *removed* from the Church?

One of the most difficult things to deal with when you are called to the office of a prophet is the rejection you receive from your brothers and sisters in Christ. When you are branded by God with this gift and calling, you not only struggle to be as accurate as possible delivering His word, but you also struggle with others standing around judging you. This makes it doubly tough.

There will be those who listen to your words to find something that, in their doctrine or opinion, is not of God so they can tag you as a false prophet. It's difficult enough to be a Christian in a world that is rapidly turning into heathens without having your own kind wanting to stone you. However, things have loosened up a bit in a few churches, and there are people who are curious enough to secretly cross their denominational boundaries and ask for a word from one of the many prophetic people in the world today.

When I started in 1989, there were a few pastors and lay ministers who wanted me punished for even thinking I was called to the office of a prophet. I admit that in the earlier times it did sound very self-serving to call yourself a prophet of God. Let's face it: those who were known to call themselves a prophet of God were people like David Koresh, the Wacko prophet from Waco, Texas, or Jim Jones, the Kool-Aid prophet. Both of these men led their followers to their ultimate deaths. Back then I could not help but feel as though God were playing some sick joke, placing the

191

mantle of a prophet around my neck only to have good Christian folks wanting to hang me with it.

No wonder I became known as the "Mail-Order Prophet." It seemed to be the safest way to do what God was calling me to do and still maintain some quality of life. It was brutal enough trying to break into the churches and ministerial alliances around the country during those earlier times.

For the first 3 years I was in the ministry, not once was I received in a local church; although, God had me ministering 6 days a week somewhere. We had a live radio program where I prophesied live over the radio as the lines were open for callers. People would also set up meetings for me in their homes, bank buildings, hotel ball rooms, and many other unorthodox places. I wondered how long it would be before I could minister in a church building.

"So they were offended at Him. But Jesus said to them, 'A prophet is not without honor except in his own country and in his own house'" (Matt. 13:57).

When I first read this verse, I realized this is one of the promises of the Bible. Not many would want to claim this verse for themselves. However, if you are called of God to the office of a prophet, then it helps you to understand why these things are happening to you. With this verse of scripture in mind, I began to ask God to send me outside of the area, which He did. The first place God opened up to me was Hawaii, and there I was received with open arms.

The very first week I was on the island of Oahu, I was proph-esying live over television. On the first day, calls flooded the sta-tion, and the owners called the phone company to get a count of how many calls they had missed in the 30 minutes I was on the air. There were 11 telephones in the television station and all were being answered, but according to the phone company we still missed 258 calls while the lines were all busy.

From there, God sent me to Norway with the same over-whelming acceptance that I had in Hawaii the month before. Then on to Sweden, England, Thailand, Denmark, and many other countries all with open arms, starving for a prophetic encounter, believing God could speak through a simple, broken vessel such as me. For the next 2 ½ years, I was out of the country for three weeks out of every month.

This just proves that the promises of God are real; however, you do not have the choice to just pick one out and claim it for yourself. It might not be the one He has for you.

How to Know the Signs from God

"The first man was of the earth, made of dust; the second Man is the Lord from Heaven. As was the man of dust, so also are those who are made of dust; and as is the heavenly Man, so also are those who are heavenly" (1 Cor. 15:47–48).

Looking at what has happened on Earth in the past, we find evidence that many times a prophetic prelude will show how

193

the natural world is paralleling the spiritual realm, thus the prelude creates a manifesto for the Church. There are valuable prophetic signs to be gained through these natural events. The Holy Scriptures have revealed to us a way to read the signs, forecasting what is ahead of us: "However, the spiritual is not first, but the natural, and afterward the spiritual" (1 Cor. 15:46).

There have been hundreds of thousands of young men and women who have signed their names on the dotted line to fight in the wars in Iraq and Afghanistan. Many of them signed up for the opportunity to obtain a higher education or receive an income that they could not make in the civilian world.

Many members of our military found themselves in the midst of something they did not think they had signed up for, yet they served with all that was within them. Still, others signed up just to fight for what they believed in.

As these wars begin to fade away, we can see through our nation's rearview mirror that very little was accomplished, if anything at all. What we do see is a massive loss of life and property and the demise of our way of life. Pondering the peak of our nation's pain, it is clear that we became highly motivated by anger, fear, vengeance, and greed. All of these emotions were triggered by 9/11.

So what have we learned, and what could we have done differently in order to turn tragedy into a positive mark in our nation's history? Is it possible that we could have handled this event with a heart of love rather than of hate, and had victory without the loss of lives, limbs, and minds? All without sacrificing our best, bravest, and brightest? We now have before us a chance to redirect the destiny of all godly nations in the world. However, we must first look deeper into the sign that has been played out since 2001 in order to properly forecast what direction the Holy Spirit wants to take God's people.

Now, the people of God whose names have been written into the Book of Life are being called up to fight a different kind of war: a spiritual war. When we stood up for Jesus we may have thought we were going to get a free ride. Not so! We are now being called upon to serve in His supernatural force, fighting a much different kind of foe.

For many years prior to 9/11, we experienced peace and prosperity. We enjoyed the preaching and being caught up in the praise and worship, and the fellowship at all the potlucks and other such events. Now we are at a place and time where God is calling His people to unify into an army, joined together and empowered by His love. We are already seeing a manifestation of His power. There are signs that reveal we are gaining forces from within through laying down our old traditions and fears and welcoming the Holy Spirit to come in and lead His Church into this new approach to spiritual warfare.

If you are in this movement of God, you can easily see a surge of power being released from the Holy Spirit as it is being poured into the followers of Jesus Christ, our Lord and Savior. In the natural, we are seeing a mass exodus from non-spiritual church groups. People are being led by the Holy Spirit into the baptism of Jesus, as spoken of in Acts 19:1–7. Those who have been ministering for a number of years are experiencing a huge increase in miracles, healings, revelations of knowledge, and shocking responses to our prayers.

The Church and its leaders are not the only ones who will be on the front lines in this spiritual war. From the newly born-again child of God, to the oldest and most mature godly leaders, we will be mixing it up with the enemy; however, our weapons are not of this world. Like I have mentioned—this is a new approach to dealing with spiritual warfare. Looking at the errors made in the natural war, we can learn from this sign from God as to how to obtain victory in this spiritual war against our enemies.

In a natural war, you look at everything with your natural eye. It is much different when you are involved in spiritual wars. To be honest, most of the past spiritual battles the church has been through have not been so successful, and I am about to tell you why. Our enemy cannot be viewed as a human or a nation. "For we do not wrestle against flesh and blood, but against principalities, against powers, against the rulers of the darkness of this age, against spiritual hosts of wickedness in the heavenly places" (Eph. 6:12).

There is one reason why so many of the church's battles never seem to be victorious. Some battles have been over such topics as abortion, same sex marriage, serving in the military, violence on television and video games, and a number of other saber-rattling convictions the church has cried out against. I could take them one by one and go into great detail, but let me just try to give you the gist of why our methods have not worked.

First and foremost, the greatest problem within the church is that the mainstream, or majority of the Body of Christ, does not believe anyone can really talk to God and receive a clear answer or direction. This ignorance says to me that many within the mainstream do not believe what is written in the Bible, for everything in the Bible is about hearing God. Without consulting our Heavenly Father about what we should do, someone starts a battle cry against a group or issue. They get the idea that all Christians don't like what is happening in the world and they decide to declare war on their own. If you are not going to seek God for His approval to go to war on an issue, you will always lose!

It's All about the Attitude

The second thing that has kept the Body of Christ from being victors in the eyes of the world and our Heavenly Father is our attitude. The Church should not be the manic macho group that goes around condemning and judging the world. We are NOT called to judge the ways of the world. The commandments from our Lord are very clearly stated: we are not of it and we are not to rule over it. It belongs to a different ruler, Satan himself.

Jesus commands His Church, "Therefore be merciful, just as your Father also is merciful. Judge not, and you shall not be judged.

Condemn not, and you shall not be condemned. Forgive, and you will be forgiven" (Luke 6:36–37). We are not called to judge the world; however, we are to hold those of us in the Church accountable to what is right and just in the eyes of God, according to His word.

"And if anyone hears my words and does not believe, I do not judge him; for I did not come to judge the world but to save the world" (John 12:47). It pays to obey the convictions within our heart, even when we do not think we have done anything wrong, for it is the Holy Spirit who is judging us. Therefore, we need to pray the prayer of forgiveness.

"When we are judged, we are chastened by the Lord, that we may not be condemned with the world" (1 Cor. 11:32).

On the other hand, we are to judge ourselves as well as those who are in the Body of Christ. The protocol for how to judge other believers is very clear. The biblical order for having someone's inappropriate lifestyles or heinous actions judged and dealt with can be found in Matthew 18:15–20. There are leaders within the Body of Christ who are anointed and chosen by our Lord, who have the power to make final judgments within the Body of Christ.

Jesus commissioned His disciples in John 20:21–23, "'Peace to you! As the Father has sent Me, I also send you.' And when He had said this, He breathed on them, and said to them, 'Receive the Holy Spirit. If you forgive the sins of any, they are forgiven them; if you retain the sins of any, they are retained.'"

We even see in 1 Timothy 1:15–18 where God empowered leaders who demonstrated their power by enforcing the commandment on Earth as it was declared in Heaven. There are proper settings for governing the church that is established and ordained by God. There is an order for handling individuals or groups of believers according to these scriptures and their examples.

Terrestrial Christians vs. Celestial Christians

ID of a Terrestrial Christian: one who is born-again and saved from eternal damnation and baptized in the baptism of repentance. They have a form of godliness but are "unloving, unforgiving, slanderers, without self-control, brutal, despisers of good, traitors, headstrong, haughty, lovers of pleasure rather than lovers of God, having a form of godliness but denying the power" (2 Tim. 3:3–4). They don't believe in the baptism of the Holy Spirit, or that spiritual gifts are for today. These types of Christians rarely help the church and seem to enjoy coming against everyone outside of their own congregations.

ID of a Celestial Christian: Christians who have been born-again, saved from eternal damnation, baptized in water, the baptism of repentance (also known as the baptism of John the Baptist). These Christians have also been empowered by the baptism of the Holy Spirit, also known as the baptism of Jesus Christ.

Not all Christians are the same and we are not all equal. How could we think that we all have received from God the same blessings, beauty, intelligence, humor, talents, and even spiritual gifts? Life is not fair and we are not all equal. Although, it sounds good to tell everyone they are all equal, and you have been told at some point that God has no favorites. Then what about King David, a man after God's own heart? His son Solomon, the richest man in the world in his day and forevermore, as recorded in the Bible? What matters to God is what you do with all that He has given you in this life.

You may be living the most horrible life one can imagine. If so, I encourage you to be an overcomer and stretch yourself to do more than anyone expects you to do. Then even God will notice and reward you. We are rewarded by what we do, not by who we are. Your eternal blessing could be the greatest in all of Heaven, depending on what you do with what God gave you while you were on this Earth. Jesus has told us, "Take heed what you hear. With the same measure you use, it will be measured to you; and to you who hear, more will be given" (Mark 4:24).

You see, it's easy to begin climbing out of your slump, depression, financial problems, health problems, or whatever else is holding you down. All you have to do is pray, hear, and obey. With this one principle you will receive life more abundant, as Jesus promised us in this life as well as in the life to come (see John 10:10b). If you do all that the Lord asks of you, He will continue to reward you even when all others reject you.

"There are also celestial bodies and terrestrial bodies; but the glory of the celestial is one, and the glory of the terrestrial is another. There is one glory of the sun, another glory of the moon, and another glory of the stars; for one star differs from another star in glory" (1 Cor. 15:40–41).

No matter how small or insignificant you might think of yourself, remember that you are a very important part of God's plan for His Church. If you are a Celestial Christian, you will follow the call of God upon your life and the Church will prosper because of you. The Body is only functioning at 100% when all the members are operating in unity, synced together by the power of God's love for this lost and self-destructing world.

Our Weapons for Spiritual Warfare

Maybe you remember the day in Iraq when our troops and allies entered Baghdad. It was considered a major victory. In the natural realm this would be true. However, looking at the spiritual side, the victory came when our troops tied a cable around the statue of Saddam Hessian and toppled it to the ground. This was a sign from God that we too will be taking down idols and major strongholds that stand against the Son of God. The Holy Spirit is increasing our power and distributing His weapons of warfare to knock down wicked idols, and not just in the natural. He is going to start knocking down idols even in your own homes.

Our weapons are listed in 1 Corinthians 12:1–11, the nine spiritual gifts of the Holy Spirit, and in Romans 12:3–8, which lists various ministries afforded to us to accomplish God's will, to win the battle against the devil who comes to steal, kill, and destroy (John 10:10). We sharpen our weapons and train daily to perfect a LOVE for the lost souls by practicing these nine acts of God, which give us the power of the Holy Spirit to win the sinner. The sinner will always be controlled by the devil and will win in any conflict when you try to use their weapons of warfare. We can never win any battle when we try to use the devil's weapons: anger, vengeance, boasting, fighting, swearing, killing, destroying, mocking, or murdering.

These are the weapons of a Celestial Christian: "But the fruit of the Spirit is love, joy, peace, longsuffering, kindness, goodness, faithfulness, gentleness, self-control. Against such there is no law and those who are Christ's have crucified the flesh with its passions and desires" (Gal. 5:22–24). With the gifts, power, fruit, and calling upon our individual lives, we can turn this old world back to its rightful owners, God the Father, God the Son, and God the Holy Spirit.

What Will God Do for You?

We are now going into a new time of life in America, changed forever by the war that began September 11, 2001. Things are going to change even more in the market place, in business, governments, and education. The church must change too. At present, our Lord has our prophetic elders busy writing a new course of direction for the church's protocol and code of ethics. In accordance with what the Lord has revealed through His prophets, an effort is being made to revitalize the direction of the Church to protect the Body of Believers and empower the Body to overcome their enemies.

Chapter 11

Knowing the Things of God

W hen I finally surrendered to the calling on my life, I began to really study the bible. The one thing that kept grabbing me was that we should be able to hear the voice of God and have the power to minister in spiritual gifts. The only way I knew to obtain these gifts was to ask for them. So every morning at 5:45, I would go to the church sanctuary and walk and pray for an hour or more each day.

After about 8 to 10 weeks of faithfully praying and asking God to be used in signs and wonders, He spoke to me. Now, this was not some faint whisper I heard. It was His audible voice booming in this wide open space. He started with this exact question: "Do you want to do the stuff?" Without thinking, I responded with a loud "YES," wondering why it had taken so long for Him to hear my prayers. He then interrupted my thoughts, saying: "Then love my people the way I do."

I took a quick self-examination of my abilities to love people like Jesus loved the people and realized I couldn't do that of myself. So from that day forward I changed my prayer to: "Lord, teach me how to love your people the way you do."

Within just a couple of weeks of that, I was invited to travel with a group of apostles and prophets who were scheduled to travel through Texas to minister in a number of churches. It was at the very first church we visited that Prophet Gary Brooks prophesied and laid hands upon me to receive the spiritual gifts of prophecy, the word of knowledge, and the word of wisdom.

"For the gifts and the calling of God are irrevocable" (Rom. 11:29).

It is true that when God blesses you with a spiritual gift it is irrevocable. In other words, it cannot be taken away. Many folks have a real problem with this, but He will not take the gift back if misused. He simply removes the vessel. That is something to truly fear. The scripture above also gives an explanation as to why the gift is still working when ministers go astray, living a life in sin but still ministering in the spiritual gift for which they are known. Unfortunately, there are also ministers who lead God's people with an iron fist and make demands of their flock that are unreasonable.

Those kinds of misgivings concerned me for years until the Holy Spirit taught me about these truths regarding spiritual gifts. After I had received the prophetic gifts, my life was radically changed. However, at the same time I was troubled over what our Lord Jesus had said in this verse: "Not everyone who says to me,

'Lord, Lord,' shall enter the kingdom of Heaven, but he who does the will of My Father in Heaven. Many will say to me in that day, 'Lord, Lord, have we not prophesied in your name, cast out demons in your name, and done many wonders in your name?' And then I will declare to them, 'I never knew you; depart from me, you who practice lawlessness!'" (Matt. 7:21–23).

In the beginning of this ministry, I thought that I could do no wrong in the eyes of God. Soon, however, these verses shattered me and made me question my own salvation; I wondered how I would ever be sure that I was pleasing God. Even while ministering in the gifts of the Holy Spirit, I could mess up and hear Him say, "Turn from me, I don't know you." How could I ever get it right? What must I do to please God and not feel at risk of losing my position in Heaven? It seemed to take years before the Holy Spirit came to me and told me what I needed to do to keep myself safe in the eyes of God. What He said is easy to repeat but much more difficult to accomplish. Once again, these were His words: "Love My people the way I do."

Abiding in God's Will

"If you abide in me, and my words abide in you, you will ask what you desire, and it shall be done for you" (John 15:7).

This verse of scripture has a much deeper meaning than you may think. To "abide in me" is to live in Christ and Him in you, and you are forbidden to meditate or touch anything that is not of Him. This part of the verse is not too difficult to understand because anything of sin should not be let in.

It's the next part of the verse that has been misunderstood for a long time by many and needs further explanation—"and my words abide in you." Here is what most people think this part of the verse is saying: if you stay away from sin and read your bible every day, or as often as possible, then you are abiding in His word. Therefore, their belief is that the promise in this verse in John 15, "you will ask what you desire, and it shall be done for you," is automatically working for every believing Christian. When it doesn't work in their life, they question their faith and the truth of the bible.

We must be willing to answer the call of the Holy Spirit and be willing to follow Him to the depths of our sanity. He will take you through various situations along this journey, teaching you what His words really mean. Whether it's the written word or the spoken word, we must obtain understanding because this will increase our knowledge; and with knowledge we will become much wiser.

Now let's give this some thought. It's not too difficult to read your bible and restrain yourself from offending God, so why doesn't every Christian receive whatever they so desire? After all, the bible promises it to be so. The promise in this verse we are discussing states that "you will ask what you desire, and it shall be done for you."

This is a very powerful promise and I will explain how you are to obtain it. Know that the first part of this puzzle of truth must be broken down in order for us to see the prerequisites outlined within it. When we do this, we can receive the full measure of the promise and its manifestation. Allow me, if you will, to stretch your faith a little and share with you what I have been taught by the Holy Spirit. The next few steps are not meant to offend, but rather to help set you in a place to begin walking in the fullness of the promises of God.

Remember this one thing: the Holy Bible is 100% from God and is all true! Truth will always work when applied as instructed. If what you have been taught in the past is not working, then it is not being taught correctly and it is time to ask the only true Teacher for the correct answers. The Holy Spirit is the author and teacher that will give you all truth and nothing but the truth. Also, remember that what is written in the Holy Bible is not all there is to know about living this life as a child of God. We can continue to learn daily from our God, for He is NOT dead but alive and He is speaking to you and me.

Who or What is the Word of God?

First of all, your bible is not the Word of God. Jesus Christ is the Word of God, and He can speak to you through the written words found in the bible. Do not be confused—He is not wood pulp and ink, bound in genuine leather. The Holy Scriptures are a compilation of divine events that are inscribed testimonials about God the Father, God the Son, and God the Holy Spirit.

When you are reading from your bible, you need to know the difference between the logos word and His Rhema Word. Many words in the bible have more than one meaning, for they originated in another language than English. When we read our bibles in the English translation, the same word can be used over and over and have the same meaning. However, in the original text it may have had multiple meanings.

If you are reading your bible and you are just obtaining information as you study, you are reading the written word (or the logos word). The Holy Spirit can use any book, billboard, poster, man, woman, child, and even a donkey to speak to you. There is no limit to how God can speak His Rhema Word (or His life-giving word). We are always looking for the life-giving word, the Rhema Word of God. The Rhema Word changes our lives, gives us direction, heals, and delivers us. Do you know what it's like to have the Holy Spirit speak His Rhema Word to you in the very hour you have need?

This is the Rhema Word this verse is talking about, not just whatever you want to read or claim for yourself. The verse is referring to the Rhema Word from Jesus Christ, who IS the living Word in this verse. "If you abide in me, and my words abide in you, you will ask what you desire, and it shall be done for you."

I hope and pray you understand this part and use it as your spiritual compass to guide you through life. Continually keep your spiritual antennas up, ready to receive every life-giving Rhema Word that comes to you. It is your Master, King, Lord Jesus speaking to you. Pray, hear, and obey, for it is the Christian way!

Hear and Obey, or Go Your Own Way

Jesus is not dead. He is alive and speaking to you and me. The problem is that we have become dull of hearing. We have become so involved in what the world has to offer with all of its noise, its propaganda, and its advertisements, that it has become difficult to know God's perfect will for our lives. The Holy Spirit is always trying to speak to us over the noise of this world and He wants to tell us what's to come in our future—if we will only hear Him.

By hearing a prophecy from a prophet, you will have the unction and desire to hear God for yourself. How will we be able to know except there is one given to us to hear God for us? One of the ways God speaks to us is by revealing His will through personal prophecy. This can reveal things that only God would know because no other one would know the person's situation. By hearing a prophecy from a prophet or prophetic minister, you will have the unction and desire to hear God for yourself.

God is speaking to us Spirit to spirit. "Likewise the Spirit also helps in our weaknesses. For we do not know what we should pray for as we ought, but the Spirit Himself makes intercession for us with groanings which cannot be uttered. Now He who searches the hearts knows what the mind of the Spirit is, because He makes intercession for the saints according to the will of God" (Rom. 8:26–27).

The disciples said to Jesus, "Speak plainly, we do not understand you! You speak in parables, saying things that are confusing."
If the disciples who walked with Jesus in the flesh could not comprehend what He was saying, how much more difficult is it for
you and me to understand? We who are born of the Spirit must
hear Him who is Spirit. It is a challenge, and it is not something
you can just begin to do. It has to happen to you before you begin
to understand. When it happens to you, you will have a choice of
whether you will hear and obey or go your own way.

Obedience is the Way

It is not our sacrifice or our works that God wants from us, but
it is our obedience of what He wants us to do. It is through obedience that all of the blessings of God come to us. Were you not
called by God to confess Jesus to be His only begotten Son, and
Lord and Savior for all mankind? Was it not by the conviction
of the Holy Spirit that you knew within yourself that you were a
sinner? It was only possible when the Holy Spirit spoke to you
and gave you the choice to receive Him as Lord and Savior, or
not to receive Him.

Do you know that the Holy Spirit wants to speak to you today?
He wants to speak to you and tell you about all the good things He
wants to do in your life. He also wants to give you instruction so
that you can receive all the blessings that He has in store for you.

The Lord wants you to pray, hear, and obey; how else will you know what you are to do for Jesus and His kingdom?

Jesus said He did nothing by his own authority. He only did what He saw the Father do and spoke only what the Father told Him to say. That is the Christian way! Jesus knew how to follow the Father because His instructions were written on the tablets of Jesus' heart by the very finger of God (see Proverbs 7:3). Did you know that God wants to seal His instructions on the tablets of YOUR heart? He will do it when you begin to fervently pray, hear, and obey.

The Yo-yo Way

Many people fail to receive the things of God because of three primary reasons:

1. They refuse to take the time to pray and ask the Holy Spirit what He desires them to do.
2. After they have prayed and received the word of the Lord, they do not seek Him for confirmation.
3. They step out into their own decisions, failing to obey the instructions He has given them, only to find everything falling apart as they attempt to do it their own way or the way they think is best.

We can get in this yo-yo experience where God has asked us to do something that we do not want to do, so we take our lives back and do it our own way. It's like we are stomping through His blood at the cross to take back the life we supposedly gave Him. Whose life is it anyway? God said, "My servants will humble themselves and pray. Give yourself unto me and watch what I shall do for you." You have to be willing to go all the way. No matter what the cost, or fears you may have!

Unfortunately, most people today want Christ only for prosperity, a mate, and a fine life. That is not the proper exchange. You must give Him your whole life for whatever He wants to do with you. It does not matter if you suffer in the process because you will suffer in the name of Christ. What a great reward that is in store for those who suffer in His name! The outcome is His. When He is through with your life, you will be much more complete and your life will be better than you could ever have imagined. There are things He wants to bring out of us. There are things that He wants to strip from us. He wants to turn that mirror around to let us see how He sees us and how others look at us. When we have truly given our lives to Him, we will find ourselves blessed far greater than if we had done it our own way.

However, the devil would have you believe that our Heavenly Father will ask too much of you. I tell you the truth; Satan is a liar and the truth cannot be found in him. He is the father of lies. Do not believe him!

Jesus is the Word of God

"You search the Scriptures, for in them you think you have eternal life; and these are they which testify of me. But you are not willing to come to me that you may have life" (John 5:39–40).

You cannot study the scriptures like you study any other book. You must let the Holy Spirit take you into the Holy Scriptures where He wants to teach you. Jesus' Spirit is alive, and He is still speaking to us today. He can speak from the Holy Scriptures; however, there are a few who take the liberty to make the book say what they want it to say.

Throughout the ages, men have tried to change His written word by inserting their own interpretation. There are still ministers today who bypass portions of the Bible, taking editing privileges, as if they are the author of this Holy instrument, twisting and manipulating Scriptures to fit their own doctrine.

I have found that those who pray while seeking truth are led by the Holy Spirit through the Scriptures. The Holy Spirit confirms His Word throughout the Bible. If you can systematically find the constant connection from Genesis to Revelation, you will discover the thread of truth that is craftily weaved throughout the 66 masterpieces, collectively called the Holy Bible. The bottom line is that you cannot know the truth within the Bible without hearing and knowing the Holy Spirit. He is truth and He is the author of this living will and testament, distributing it to the heirs of His inheritance, through His gifts and promises that are sealed by His blood.

"He was clothed with a robe dipped in blood, and His name is called The Word of God" (Rev. 19:13).

Those who choose to reject the Holy Spirit, or who cannot receive His baptism, miss out on so much of what Jesus promised us. I thought for a number of years that I had received the baptism of the Holy Spirit. I remember when I was baptized at the age of ten; my pastor said, as he lowered me into the water, "I baptize you in the Name of the Father, the Son, and the Holy Spirit."

It wasn't until I was an adult that I learned about the Holy Spirit. My dad asked if I wanted to go to a Full Gospel Business Men's Fellowship to have dinner and listen to a businessman speak. At the time, I was a bank president, and thought to myself, "Why not? I might have the opportunity to meet some business people."

The meeting was held in a banquet room in a very expensive hotel. I met a few people, and then they called the meeting to order. They introduced the speaker, and he began telling us about his life as a successful businessman who was living the life of the rich and famous. Then he started having problems in his business, and then his wife left him. Because of this, he turned to God and was introduced to the Holy Spirit.

I thought, "That was a strange thing to say. How are you introduced to the Holy Spirit?" Since my denomination did not ever teach anything about the subject, I didn't even know there was such a thing as the Holy Spirit. The speaker kept on talking, and I was very interested in what he was saying; however, it was all foreign to me.

The speaker closed his message by asking those who were in need of prayer to come forward so that he could pray for them. The line started growing, and to my surprise, my dad was in the line. Frankly, I did not even know he was a Christian. This was a very strange but educational evening.

As I was listening to the speaker pray over various people, one businessman kneeled down next to my chair and began telling me all these things that the Holy Spirit had told him to write down about me. Then he started reading what he had written. As he walked away, I thought to myself, "This fellow is way out there." I found it to be rather humorous!

Turning back toward the prayer line, I noticed that my dad was lying flat on the floor. Seeing this shocked me because my dad would never lay down in one of his fine suits, but there he was on the floor. I wondered, "Why is no one helping him? Can't they see something is wrong?"

I jumped up and made my way to see if Dad was all right, but someone grabbed me by the arm and pulled me into the prayer line. I voiced my concern for my dad, and he assured me that he was just fine, saying that he was slain in the Spirit. Now, that just did it for me! This place was off the chart, and who were these people?

My time finally came, and I was standing right before the speaker. The first thing he asked me was, "Are you baptized in the Holy Spirit?" Well, I knew he must be referring to what my pastor had said over me as he baptized me at the age of ten, so I said that I had been.

One of my dad's friends was standing next to me, shaking his head side to side as if to say, with no uncertain body language, "No, he is not!"

I started to explain to the speaker, but he said, "Shut up." He put his hand on my shoulder. Now, when he said that, I knew within myself that it had to be God speaking through him. Don't make me explain it because I can't! Let's just say that I knew in it in my "knower."

After the man prayed for me, I had a hunger for more of God. I was going to find out how to get baptized in the Holy Spirit, if it was the last thing I did!

Knowing His Will

"But the anointing which you have received from Him abides in you, and you do not need that anyone teach you; but as the same anointing teaches you concerning all things, and is true, and is not a lie, and just as it has taught you, you will abide in Him" (1 John 2:27).

His Word rightly divides those who know about Him from those who really know Him. His anointing will guide you through the bible, teaching you His will for your life as well as imparting things into your spiritual DNA. He will brand your heart with the calling He has for your life.

After the Full Gospel Business Men's meeting I attended where my dad was slain in the Spirit, and I shortly afterwards received the real baptism of the Holy Spirit, I jumped into God's favorite game—hide and seek. When I was lost, He found me, saved me, and filled me with the Holy Ghost. Now it was my turn to go find Him, and I had many questions to ask. Since that day, I have learned so much. I try my best to share what I have learned in my quest for truth.

One of the things I have learned, looking through His eyes, is that the majority of the Body of Christ worships the Bible rather than Him whom the books of the Bible are about. I don't know about you, but my Jesus is not wood pulp and ink, bound in genuine leather. In fact, I never refer to the Bible as the Word of God. I reference this wonderful and most powerful book as the Holy Scriptures, just the same as Jesus did.

How you use the Holy Scriptures will determine whether you are living the abundant life Jesus promised or not. Some are compelled to take up arms with the bible and use it to slice and dice other Christians in the attempt to remove the splinter from their spiritual sibling's eye. These people struggle, wondering, "Why am I hurting so badly even though I faithfully tithe and give offerings?" The devourer continues to eat away, and they don't know why.

Going to their bibles, they begin to rigorously re-study, making sure they have been following the "formulas" correctly, as well as the multiple steps they have been taught. Frustrated and confused, their hearts become an easy target for Satan's fiery darts of doubt and disbelief.

The famous line from the old movie City Slickers comes to mind. Remember when the old rugged cowboy said, "All you need to know is one thing." Well, these days everyone wants to know, "What is the one thing that will make me happy again?"

I am here to tell you what that one thing is that will give you peace and happiness in this life, even if the herd has been scattered and you're lost in the wild wilderness. As we journey together in these surroundings of unknown territory, you can find His divine abundance in the midst of a world that is going madly into an abyss of debacle and decay.

It always comes down to what He is saying to you TODAY. Not what He said to someone else, or the testimonies you have read about Jesus in the Bible. You must go to Him for what you need, or at least find out how to seek Him. Don't tell me you cannot hear Him and know His will. You can! I will tell you how. It's not that you can't hear Him; it's just that you have not been taught how to find Him.

How many times have you heard a preacher give a wonderful testimony of how Jesus saved him from financial bankruptcy, turned him around, and gave him everything he asked for? You wished it would happen the same way for you! Don't go and do exactly what that preacher did, because that won't work for you. Learn how to find Him on your own and He will give you what He wants you to have, but there may be times you need someone to hear God for you because you are so emotionally involved that you're unable to hear clearly through all the noise in your head.

For years I have heard very good and powerful ministers say that if we can get His written Word down into our spirits, then we will have the authority to speak the Word, and thus we will have whatever we ask. They mean well, but their instruction is backwards. Instead of first getting God's Word in your head, and then down to your spirit, it needs to go the other way around—from your spirit first, then to your head.

In order to receive true revelation knowledge, you must first pray. If you know how to pray, then pray through until you know without a doubt your prayer has been heard. Then just go about your day! At some point when you least expect it, His Word will come to you.

Then, ask Him to confirm His word. Most of the time He will lead you to His written Word, and there you will find your confirmation. This is because He will lead you right where you are to read. Once you have your confirmation, you need to obey by doing what He has impressed upon you or spoken to you. Truth will always work. So if what you are doing is not working for you, you need to find His way. I know this way works, for I have been practicing it, and teaching others, and it does work! We all agree that this is the way He intended it to be.

Our mission is to Pray, Hear, and Obey—for this is the Christian way.

Remember what Jesus has said, "Come to me and you will find life." I believe He is speaking of the good life and its abundance. -Amen, so be it!

Jesus said, "Seek first the kingdom of God and His righteousness, and all these things shall be added to you" (Matt. 6:33).

Chapter 12

True Identity Will Erase the Myths

W hen I was a child, I would round up a couple of my little friends and we would find a good spot to lie down in the grass and watch the clouds. This cloud watching became a game of charades as we'd take turns guessing what a cluster of clouds looked like. It wasn't too long before I noticed that not everyone was seeing what I was seeing. The colors I saw were different, and I was seeing strange objects moving fast from one cloud to another. The fact that no one else was seeing the same things I was made me feel like something was wrong with me, so I would suggest that we play a different game. However, I did not forget to ask God at night before falling off to sleep, "Why do you want me to see these things?"

Recently as I was praying, I was watching the clouds and I began to see through the thin portion of the clouds a metallic glimmer of a "UFO." It seems they were purposely displaying themselves just enough for me to see a portion of their various forms. As they pulled in and out from behind the edge of a fluffy cloud, it appeared that they were spying on all of us below. Seeing them, and knowing they knew I could see them, my mind immediately took me back to times in my youth when I would ask the same questions of God: "What are these objects and why I am seeing them?"

Many times as a child I would talk to God, asking Him questions about things like sticker burs that hurt when you would step on them with your bare feet. What about ants? Why did you create ants that bite and hurt us? His answer was that in the beginning, He did not plan on making these types of discomforts for our world. I replied, "Well, what made you change your mind?"

He said, "I had little trust in mankind because Adam and Eve chose to believe Satan rather than me." I asked Him what He meant, and He began to teach me that mankind has a will to believe who they want to believe. Those who believe the lies of Satan eventually discover that God's voice is the only voice to believe and obey. Understanding this one thing helped me throughout all my years to know whatever voice you choose to follow will determine what type of life you will live.

"But the Helper, the Holy Spirit, whom the Father will send in My name, He will teach you all things, and bring to your remembrance all things that I said to you" (John 14:26).

How wise our heavenly Father truly is! Over the years, He has taught me to think about things in a much different way. Learning how to see around the corner to tomorrow is a huge advantage for anyone to have, especially during hard times. The vast majority of people seem to believe that hearing the Holy Spirit is reserved for only those who are written about in the Bible.

Even among the Spirit-filled Christians, many believe He only speaks to ministers or other elect, but this is simply not so. In fact, He has been speaking to you all your life; you just need someone to show you when He is speaking and how to tune your ear to His voice. Once you know when and how He has been speaking to you, the Holy Spirit begins bringing to your remembrance all the times He has spoken throughout your life.

As I recall, much of my early childhood was spent lying in my small twin bed seeking God's voice. Every time I asked Him a question, He would answer me with another question. This forced me to stop and think. With due thought, I would always receive from Him more than just the answer to my question. With the knowledge I received from His question, I would gain understanding.

One night when I was about 6 years old and unable to sleep, I asked God, "Why did you make feet so ugly?"

In just a second or two, He responded, "How would you have made them?"

As I struggled with how I would have made feet, I became frustrated that all my thoughts generated around objects that had already been made. Chicken feet, horse hooves, and bear paws were coming to my mind as I began imagining how I would have made human feet.

Finally, I grew weary and fell asleep. I learned that night that nothing is new, not even the ideas we receive are new. All that can be created is already here. Also, His answer to my question led me to understand that everything that He has created is beautiful, and that anything else to replace it would only bear the mark of a counterfeit.

This reminds me of an old joke about three scientists who decided that they were smart enough to create a man. They came to the brilliant conclusion (after reading the first book of the bible) that all they needed was to obtain some dirt from various parts of the world.

As they stood before all the different mounds of soil, preparing to make a human, God said, "OH, NO! You make your own dirt!" The men knew then that they would not succeed.

This story reveals that even the simplest of things in life cannot be re-created without God. However, when His Word abides within us, we can make anything we may need if we have His faith and the desire to believe.

"Jesus said, 'If you abide in me, and my words abide in you, you will ask what you desire, and it shall be done for you'" (John 15:7).

Even as we get older, we should never stop asking God questions. After all these years, I still have questions about many things. Over the years I have encountered angels as well as demons, though I prefer only to have visitations from angels. There is so much to learn about angels. For example, cherubs are not fat little baby angels. A cherub is a special craft that is used for transporting. (You will find out later much more about the functions of a cherub from verses in the bible.)

If you have ever seen a cherub or an angel, you will never forget it. They are very difficult to explain. If you have read the book of Ezekiel, who was a prophet of God, you will see in chapters 1 and 10 the difficulties he had describing what he was seeing. Also, Prophet Elijah was described as being taken up to Heaven on a chariot of fire. This analogy of a chariot of fire very well demonstrates that we can only describe UFO's or cherubs by objects that we know and use in our everyday life.

Because of our government's mass efforts to censor these sightings and encounters, along with the lack of knowledge, many Christians do not believe in such things for today. However, the Holy Bible is full of such things and the writers of it described what they saw to the best of their ability.

We all know that most people do not believe in what we call UFOs, but I know what they are. I have seen a UFO fly over Southlake, Texas, and I later learned what it was that I had seen from the Holy Spirit, who taught me from the bible.

During the summer of 1987, I was driving to work one night at about 11:00 p.m. Through my windshield, I witnessed a huge craft that was black as night slowly moving at a distance of about 100 yards over the traffic. What I saw was something unbelievable! It was a craft that was not made by man. As the craft hovered over the city, I stopped my vehicle and got out to see and listen. Under the belly of this huge craft were very dim lights, pastel in color, slowly flashing through the darkened craft.

It was huge as it hovered over the city. I took a quick visual measurement, and it was approximately 300 feet off the ground. There were three layers to this unusual flying machine. The first layer was about 300 yards wide. Then I noticed a fin-like support at the back of the first layer that was slightly angled back. This support connected to the second layer, which was smaller, and about 50 yards wide. Straining my eyes, I could see a second finned support for the third layer, which was about 700 square feet.

As I listened, I could hear musical sounds coming from the first layer. It was a sound I had never heard before and I don't even know how to describe it. It seemed like the musical sounds were praises that were coming from the first level, travelling to the top layer. On the second layer were voices, but they did not appear to be singing, only speaking to whom or whatever was on the top tier.

The huge craft suddenly stopped moving and then jerked back like it was changing gears. In a flash it took off like a bullet, leaving a swirling trail that quickly disappeared. I wanted to slap myself. I thought I might be going crazy! One thing was for sure though—I wasn't going to tell anyone because they would haul me off to the loony bin.

I went into work that night not planning on even thinking about what I had seen, much less talking to anyone about it. As the night wore on though, I could not stop thinking about what I had seen.

My biggest question was if this thing was something from the airport? Or was it from another planet? When I thought about the spiritual side of it, I immediately thought of Ephesians 6:12. "For we do not wrestle against flesh and blood, but against principalities, against powers, against the rulers of the darkness of this age, against spiritual hosts of wickedness in the heavenly places."

As I started my all-night shift at the convenient store/gas station, I could not help but think about what I had seen, meditating on scriptures that might help me identify what this huge hovering craft was. Each time I weighed out the scriptures, I kept thinking about the part in Ephesians 6:12 where it said "rulers of the darkness," but in my spirit it just did not seem right. I remembered that the music was so beautiful, sounding more like praises going up to the top tier.

Who was it on the third tier? Why was the craft all black, and what about the pastel lights glowing off and on underneath the first tier? Why were there three levels, and who was on the middle tier? We know from the Holy Scriptures that Lucifer, who we know as Satan, was the head musician in Heaven before he was cast out. I wondered if it was he who sat atop the black three-tiered craft.

About midway through my shift, one of my regular customers, who was head of security at DFW International Airport, came in. He showed up earlier than normal. As he came to the counter with his usual coffee and pastry, I asked if he had heard about anything strange happening at the airport.

He quickly raised his head and stared at me with wide eyes, then asked, "What do you mean?"

I stuttered around a bit, trying to tell him what I had seen, then he quickly gathered his breakfast without saying a word and rushed out the door. Normally, we had a good long chat each morning, but not that day! It must have been something I said, so I was kicking myself for talking about seeing the three-tiered craft. I knew better than to mention this experience. For the rest of the evening, I struggled with keeping my mouth shut and my thoughts on anything but the black hovering craft.

As usual, my 7:00 a.m. replacement did not show up to take over the first shift of the day. About the time I started wondering how much longer I would have to work, the morning DJ came on for his daily radio program. I normally listened to this guy during my drive home, and I could tell he was really excited about something that morning. He kept saying, "I can't wait to tell you all that happened to me last night."

After a short commercial, he began talking about how he and his buddies were driving by DFW International Airport and a huge black UFO appeared over it. He described it in detail, and it was the same exact craft I had seen!

My replacement for work came driving up, and I was so excited but I dare not tell him what I saw, nor what the DJ was saying. As he came barreling through the door, he immediately started telling me about the black, three-tiered craft he had seen that night about

11:00 p.m. Now I was really excited, but also very confused as to what it was that I had seen. Was it evil or good?

I began to seek God each day in prayer, asking Him about the black craft. Each day He said nothing, so I finally quit asking. After about a year went by, God showed me what the black craft was, and He told me in detail what was on each of the three tiers.

Angels behind the Clouds

So many of us in Southlake, Texas, experienced this sighting in the late summer of 1987. It was so large that the craft blocked all the light from the moon and the stars. It really was difficult to wrap our heads around what we were seeing, and I had many questions about this unknown object that slowly came across the city.

About a year later, as I was on my daily walk, our Lord spoke to me saying, "I have a birthday present for you." It was just a few days until my birthday, and I began to think of all the things He might have planned for me. On my birthday, I got my bible out to read, just like every morning, and He told me to read 2 Samuel 22.

As I read the first twenty verses, it became clear that this was what many of us had seen hovering over the city. Our Lord was sharing with me that what came over Southlake, Texas, was the same craft He rode upon during the days of David. It is recorded here in 2 Samuel where our Lord came to David's rescue to deliver him from Saul and his army of warriors.

"Then David spoke to the Lord the words of this song, on the day when the Lord had delivered him from the hand of all his enemies, and from the hand of Saul.

"And he said: 'The Lord is my rock and my fortress and my deliverer; the God of my strength, in whom I will trust. My shield and the horn of my salvation, my stronghold and my refuge. My Savior, You save me from violence. I will call upon the Lord, who is worthy to be praised. So shall I be saved from my enemies.

"When the waves of death surrounded me, the floods of ungodliness made me afraid. The sorrows of Sheol surrounded me; the snares of death confronted me. In my distress I called upon the Lord, and cried out to my God. He heard my voice from His temple, and my cry entered His ears.

"Then the earth shook and trembled; the foundations of Heaven quaked and were shaken because He was angry. Smoke went up from His nostrils, and devouring fire from His mouth; coals were kindled by it. He bowed the heavens also, and came down with darkness under His feet. He rode upon a cherub, and flew; and He was seen upon the wings of the wind. He made darkness a canopy around Him, dark waters and thick clouds of the skies. From the brightness before Him, coals of fire were kindled.

"The Lord thundered from Heaven, and the Most High uttered His voice. He sent out arrows and scattered them; lightning bolts, and He vanquished them. Then the channels of the sea were seen, the foundations of the world were uncovered, at the rebuke of the Lord, at the blast of the breath of His nostrils. He sent from above,

He took me, He drew me out of many waters. He delivered me from my strong enemy, from those who hated me; for they were too strong for me. They confronted me in the day of my calamity, but the Lord was my support. He also brought me out into a broad place; He delivered me because He delighted in me'" (2 Sam. 22:1–20).

As you might now see, this birthday gift was the understanding that I had been seeking. It was the best birthday gift ever! Not only did He lead me to these verses of Scripture, but He also began to tell me how David was surrounded and out-numbered by his enemies. There was no way he could have lived through the attack, but when God came screaming out of Heaven on His cherub with a mighty blast, He vaporized David's enemies. From the coals of fire, the flashing pale lights under the cherub, arrows fired like lasers of light, destroying everything and everyone around David. Then our Lord took David up into the cherub and delivered him to a safe place.

Everything the Lord was showing me had to do with David's experience thousands of years ago, so I asked, "What about that day in 1987?" This is when I really began to learn unknown things about many of the events written in the Holy Bible.

The Lord's cherub, black in color with three tiers, have a distinct purpose. The larger lower level of the cherub carries the 144,000 witnesses mentioned in the Bible. "Then I looked, and behold, a Lamb standing on Mount Zion, and with Him 144,000 having His Father's name written on their foreheads. And I heard a voice from Heaven, like the voice of many waters, and like the voice of loud thunder. And I heard the sound of harpists playing their harps. They sang, as it were, a new song before the throne, before the four living creatures and the elders; and no one could learn that song except the hundred and forty-four thousand who were redeemed from the earth" (Rev. 14:1–3).

Our Lord answered my question about the music I was hearing while His cherub hovered over the city of Southlake, Texas that summer. The sounds were something I had never heard before. I knew there were words being sung, but I could not make them out; it was more like the instruments were singing the words in a language all of their own. Then the Lamb of God said, "The sounds you heard were praises being sung by the 144,000 witnesses who were on the first tier of my cherub."

I had to ask the question I had posed so many times in prayer: what was on the second tier? Without hesitation, He said, "The 24 elders who collect the prayers of the saints and sing their prayers to me, while tossing the incense up before me, dispensing the fragrance of their pain and suffering."

"Now when He had taken the scroll, the four living creatures and the 24 elders fell down before the Lamb, each having a harp, and golden bowls full of incense, which are the prayers of the saints" (Rev. 5:8).

Prophetically Speaking

I know many of you think that this is all possibly made up, or that I have lost my mind. Before now, I have told this story to very few people, and when I did, I knew they would be ready to hear about it without being judgmental. Our Lord has shared this truth with me so that I could tell everyone what is ahead of us. I believe He purposely started showing me these things as a child, and confirming it again in my mid-thirties, to keep it fresh in my mind so that I could have enough knowledge to speak prophetically to you and others who have a mature and spiritual ear to hear what the Spirit of our Lord is about to do.

It is no big secret that the United States of America has turned drastically away from the things of God, and now has a burning lust to totally dehumanize mankind. Many people feel our God is just going to stand back and do nothing. They will soon find out that they are dead wrong. Remember what happened a few thousand years ago when two cities were crazed into unnatural acts of sexual immorality? They woke up one day to find it raining down brimstone (sulfur) and fire.

"Then the Lord rained brimstone and fire on Sodom and Gomorrah, from the Lord out of the heavens" (Gen. 19:24). Who did this to the people of those two cities? Our Lord from Heaven! How do you suppose He did that? If you said He came down riding upon His Cherub, you would be right.

The debauchery of these two cities was so hideous that when the angels of God came to bring Lot and his family out of the city before God's wrath was unleashed upon them, the men in the city desired to sexually abuse the angels of God.

"And they called to Lot and said to him, 'Where are the men [referring to the two angels in verses 1 & 2] who came to you tonight? Bring them out to us that we may know them carnally" (Gen. 19:5).

Not too many months from now, we will witness the visitation of the Lord's cherubs with His angels to do battle against those in our nation who have crossed the line of grace and spat upon the laws of our God. We have already begun to see the angels and cherubs protruding from behind the clouds, revealing signs and wonders. Strange sounds have been heard from the heavens as warning signs that God's wrath is near. We see many more signs from the heavens that confirm our Lord is preparing to descend upon parts of this nation and strike fear in the hearts of millions of people.

"The fear of the Lord is the beginning of knowledge, but fools despise wisdom and instruction" (Prov. 1:7).

These same types of events have happened in other times recorded in the bible, as Jesus gave power unto the apostles to knock the dust from their feet. Destruction came to those cities that did not receive them.

"And whoever will not receive you nor hear you, when you depart from there, shake off the dust under your feet as a testimony against them. Assuredly I say to you, it will be more tolerable for Sodom and Gomorrah in the Day of Judgment than for that city!" (Mark 6:11)

It is very important for every Christian to be aware of the wrath of God when it comes upon the lukewarm, as well as the cold of heart. We all need to strengthen each other with truth. There is no gray area in this matter of urgency. I am not going to worry about being politically correct here, just to please those who outwardly despise God and His Word. If God is the same yesterday, today, and forevermore, then you can be sure that the supernatural wrath of God will manifest soon. We need everyone who is sold out to God our Father to stay focused upon His Holy Spirit at all times, for at any moment He could come to you in a whisper, telling you to leave the city where you reside.

"Jesus Christ is the same yesterday, today, and forever" (Heb. 13:8).

Our Father has been known to deliver every one of His people from all the cities that continue to wallow in their depravity prior to their demise. He sends His angels to direct us away from those who are not His people. You do not want to argue or make excuses to God's messengers when they come to you with His word, giving you direction to go another way. God is faithful to send you His saving grace, but if you do not act upon it you could be in really bad trouble.

Over the past several years, I have been asked by over a hundred people if they should move out of their city and state. After talking to each one of them a few times over the phone, it became very clear that many of them were to move. It is easy to make excuses as to why you cannot move. I am here to tell you that if God has prompted you to move, then you do not need to procrastinate.

Another thing I have learned is that if God wants you to do something, He will reveal the steps for you to take in order to make it happen. Finding out these types of things from God is a large part of what I do through this ministry. There are great rewards found in helping those in need of knowing God's will. Once you know God's will, you may need someone to prophetically help you find the process for God's perfect plan in relocating. If you think you are someone who is supposed to move, then you need to partner with someone you feel really has an ear to hear God for you.

Equipping God's Generals for the Next Generation

Most all of you who have been with me for the last twenty years or longer know about the Vision of the Tabernacle. The vision I received from our Lord and Savior Jesus Christ has transposed from one direction to another, leaving me speechless, at times not knowing exactly what He was doing. Just about the time I thought I had it figured out, He would throw me a curve, stretching my thoughts in a new direction.

Now that we have come this far, a new and fresh release of His Word has us running double-time to keep up with His growing venue of revelation each day. We have waited so many years to see something happen; and now that which He shared with us in 1991 is beginning to take shape.

We are not constructing a building; however, we are building the Tabernacle of God one living stone after another. For God is more interested in His people than a building. With each person He sends our way, we immediately begin to see where each one of His selected vessels fit in the Master's plan. This includes YOU! It is also interesting that He is selecting a group of people who would not be most builder's choice. We quickly discovered that the unknown prophetic people He chooses to send our way are searching for their place in His Kingdom, and are being empowered to walk in His anointing. Jesus is the Chosen Stone and YOU are His Chosen People!

"Coming to Him as to a living stone, rejected indeed by men, but chosen by God and precious, you also, as living stones, are being built up a spiritual house, a holy priesthood, to offer up spiritual sacrifices acceptable to God through Jesus Christ. Therefore, it is also contained in the scripture, 'Behold, I lay in Zion a chief cornerstone, elect, precious, and he who believes on Him will by no means be put to shame'" (1 Pet. 2:4–6).

The End

CPSIA information can be obtained
at www.ICGtesting.com
Printed in the USA
FSOW03n0541080616
21262FS

9 781498 474894